Starting a Project

A Step-by-Step Guide on how to Plan a Project
within a corporate environment

By

Frederick King

Part of the series "Consulting-University.com"

1st edition November 2023

ISBN: 9798865333050

Book cover: Alexander Szymura

For more information, visit **www.Consulting-University.com** or send us an email to info@consulting-university.com

Imprint:

Frederick King
Ohlsdorfer Strasse 2
22299 Hamburg
Germany

Frederick King, a renowned project manager and freelance consultant, who brings his expertise to the forefront in this book. Having served as a project manager at Porsche Consulting and accumulated over a decade of consulting experience, Frederick now operates as a sought-after freelance project manager. With a portfolio of over 25 projects, this book as his first of four publications, has now been translated into English.

Unlocking Success through Project Planning and Preparation

In the dynamic corporate world of today, effective project management is the cornerstone of organizational success. Yet, numerous projects falter from the outset due to insufficient planning and preparation, leading to looming risks, accumulating delays, and escalating challenges. This book is tailored to address these issues.

The book navigates you through a range of essential topics, providing you as project managers with a compass to guide you through the murky waters of project planning and project preparation. From project goals to project scope, project sponsors to stakeholders and stakeholder analysis, project resources to project organization and project reporting to steering committees. I leave no stone unturned to empower you with the necessary knowledge and tools.

What sets this book apart from others in the field is its engaging narrative. Through the story of Michael and Robert, two fictional characters embark on a corporate project. Readers are transported into a world of practical examples and use cases. This storytelling approach adds a dynamic dimension to the learning process, allowing you to witness the intricacies of project planning unfold before your eyes. Moreover, the provided templates and checklists serve as valuable aid, ensuring that the provided knowledge can be immediately turned into actions.

It is worth noting that this book is not solely intended for experienced project managers. Its accessibility makes it equally suitable for beginners, providing them with a solid foundation upon which to build their project management skills.

A thread that weaves throughout this book is the paramount importance placed on effective communication and collaboration. By stressing the significance of setting standards and establishing clear lines of communication with stakeholders before a project commences, I highlight how misunderstandings can be avoided, paving the way for smoother project execution. Communication truly emerges as the lifeblood of successful project management, and my book serves as a beacon, guiding you toward effective strategies.

The focus of this book lies on methodology and practical application. The step-by-step framework presented, provides project managers with a blueprint to navigate the complexities of project planning. It empowers you to anticipate risks and minimize delays concerning time, budget, and quality.

I hope that you will be equipped with a comprehensive understanding of project planning's crucial facets and how they interconnect. The provision of checklists and templates for each step is a testament to their commitment to saving your time and enhancing the overall experience.

To sum up, this book is an invaluable resource for those aiming to excel in corporate and consultancy project planning and preparation. Regardless of whether you're an emerging project manager, a seasoned expert, or a consultant keen on refining your craft, the insights within will fortify your journey. Embark on this enlightening voyage, assimilate the shared knowledge, and experience the transformative power of project planning firsthand.

Frederick

Work smarter, not harder.

Notes for reading

Each chapter is dedicated to one topic and at the end of the chapter you will find "Learning Nuggets" and a checklist. The learning nuggets summarize the essential aspects of the topic. The checklist helps you to prepare your projects so that you can quickly overview and check off all aspects.

For each topic, I provide you with practice-oriented slides. These have proven themselves in practice, so you can use them intuitively for your projects. However, before you use these slides in your project, you should adapt them to your company (e.g., corporate identity for colors and fonts).

You can find many slides for free on my homepage www.Consulting-University.com. These are not all part of this book. There you will find instructions on how to copy slides correctly and add them to your master presentation of your company.

You will find a list of abbreviations and further explanations in the appendix.

Objective and target group of this book

This book aims to provide you with a tested and proven toolbox of methods to prepare projects, secure project implementation, and lead your project to success.

After reading through the book and applying all aspects to your project, you will realize that you have already avoided and anticipated many pitfalls so that later challenges and project risks have been reduced and mitigated. It helps you to put your project on a good foundation to handle later challenges and risks more easily.

The target audience of this book is primarily executives, project managers, and project members in large and medium-sized companies and corporations. In these companies, many stakeholders, departments, and different areas of responsibility must work together. This often results in challenges for the project manager. Of course, the basics, methods, and aspects can be applied to all projects regardless of the size of the company and its industry.

The contents of the book are also relevant for management consultants who want to learn the basics of project management and planning projects. Especially if you are just starting in management consulting or are still a beginner in project management, the book will offer you a good introduction to the topic. For newly promoted project managers it will explain methods and ideas so that you can apply them in your program, project, or subproject.

Furthermore, the book helps you to further develop your practical project management skills, as I provide proven methods and new food for thought.

Since I am asked again and again: All topics and aspects from this book are just as relevant for agile project management as for traditional project management. Even though we only exemplify one project in this book, all aspects can be transferred to the respective project regardless of the method.

Before diving into the content, one important aspect needs to be clarified: How formalized must a project or its management be?

By formalized, I mean how many formal rules need to be put in place, carried out, and documented so that you have fewer meetings and calls in the project execution later. Example:

You need project staff from different departments for the project, but how do you get them to work on your project?

1. You can talk to the employee, and he/she agrees to work on the project.
2. You can talk to the employee and his or her disciplinary supervisor and get verbal assurances of cooperation.
3. You can talk to the employee and his/her disciplinary superior and have the cooperation confirmed e.g., by e-mail, stating the assignment period and the employee's capacity.
4. In addition to the written confirmation under point 3, you have the cooperation and capacities of all project members confirmed in the kick-off steering committee and document these in the minutes, which are sent to all steering committee participants afterward.

While point 1 is not very formal, point 4 is very formal. The more formal the project, the more time you must spend on coordination and documentation. Nevertheless, it is worthwhile to make this extra effort upfront to spend less time on administrative tasks and renewed reconciliation meetings later in the project.

In general, therefore:

- The more hierarchical your company, the more formalized the project must be.
- The lower the hierarchical level of the project manager, the more formalized the project must be.
- The more challenges and problems that have occurred during projects in the past, the more formalized the project needs to be.
- The less project discipline is practiced in the company, the more formalized the project must be.

- In addition, all details should be approved in the first kick-off steering committee, so that you can always refer to its minutes. To avoid discussing all details in full depth and save time, you can always refer to the appendix of your presentation when making decisions. For this purpose, the steering committee presentation must be distributed in advance and with sufficient lead time. But more on this later in Chapter 7, "Prepare and conduct the first Steering Committee."

Finally, "a methodology is just a methodology." If aspects such as minutes or documentations are not used properly, do not be surprised if the project hits the wall anyway. It is up to you as the project manager to properly implement and, most importantly, enforce these methods. Especially in longer projects, a "fraying" can be observed over time, as the project discipline decreases. It is therefore up to you as project manager, PMO, and project member to live the established methods, to demand and stick to them. As soon as you as the project manager no longer live this discipline by yourself, it becomes difficult or even impossible to demand this from other project participants. This is one of the keys to successful project management and successful projects.

Definition of a Project

Before we begin the story in the next chapter, it is important that we take a closer look at the definition of a project:

I am sure, you have a definition of "project". But if we take a closer look, we realize that everyone has their idea of a project. So, it's no surprise to anyone why so many "projects" are difficult or impossible to distinguish from line activities.

According to PMI (Project Management Institute), a "project" is defined as follows:

"It's a temporary endeavor undertaken to create a unique product, service, or result.

A project is temporary in that it has a defined beginning and end in time, and therefore defined scope and resources.

And a project is unique in that it is not a line operation, but a specific set of operations designed to accomplish a singular goal. So, a project team often includes people who don't usually work together - sometimes from different organizations and across multiple geographies."

This means:

1. A project is something unique. Something that has not been done before, which means there is little to no experience, which is not regular, and which will not be repeated in this form (in the best case, at least if the project is successful). Thus, it is always an additional effort for the existing departments and employees in addition to the line organization. The project manager must be aware that many people consider such a project to be a "nuisance", as it disrupts their normal daily routines and involves additional work in whatever form. This means that the project manager always comes into the field as a supplicant, no matter how highly anchored the project is organizational.

2. In most cases, a project cannot be in just one department, as it is not part of the line activity. Thus, it requires a different form of

overarching cooperation than the line activity. Unfortunately, attempts are often made to make project decisions via classic line decision-making channels, which does not work. Therefore, the project needs a demarcation from the original hierarchy in the form of its project organization with its committees (known as steering committees). Even though this aspect must get into the heads of the decision-makers at the line level, it will never completely do.

The PMI definition implicitly addresses the aspect of uncertainty or novelty. Projects involve a change that affects a small group of employees during the project but may affect many employees after the project.

Our understanding of work quality and errors from line activities, therefore, does not fit project activities:

Line activities follow clear guidelines and processes and have a defined result that is known to everyone in the company. Line activities are mostly repetitive, which is why errors are often avoidable in day-to-day business: A posting in accounting is either correct or incorrect.

A project is new and therefore a journey into the unknown. Mistakes cannot be avoided but are important for finding the right solutions. For many aspects of the project business, there is no right or wrong, as there are a multitude of solution paths whose success is unknown at the beginning.

While errors in day-to-day business, therefore, reduce quality, "errors" in the project can increase quality.

Certainly, this aspect may confuse and even sounds paradoxical at first glance. But if we look at successful start-ups, this statement is supported by many:

"Try fast. Fail fast. Learn fast." is the motto of many successful start-ups. This philosophy is therefore also proclaimed in bestsellers such as "The Lean Start-up" by Eric Ries or "Testing Business Ideas" by Alex Osterwalder and David J. Bland.

Furthermore, this is the reason why there are so-called sprints in agile project management. This involves the iterative-incremental creation of the defined scope of services so that a fundamentally functional product is available at the end of a sprint.[1]

From this definition of a project, it can be deduced why many projects are not successfully implemented when certain elements are missing:

- If the project does not have clear goals and a defined project scope, it cannot be worked on in a goal-oriented manner. The question "What is different after successful project completion?" has proven itself in this context.
- If nothing is reconciled with other departments, there will be delays because the not involved departments will want to give their input into the project as soon as they hear about it. In addition, this can lead to delays when the project is transferred to the line organization.
- If (company) specifications and stakeholder interests are unknown, conflicts and delays will inevitably arise.

Now that we've cleared that up, I hope you enjoy the story.

―――

Learning Nuggets

o Projects are not line activities. Therefore, projects require different attention (especially from managers), different means of processing, different methods, and different committees.
o The project goal or the desired state after successful project completion must be clear to all stakeholders.

---

[1] The principles of "agile" are often misinterpreted and perceived as less "formal". However, since a functional product should be available at the end of each sprint, agile methods require discipline and create transparency.

The Characters of our journey

We embark on a journey in which two fictional characters engage in a dialogue to process their impressions and insights on project management.

A former management consultant, Michael, starts his new job as a project manager in the in-house consulting department of a medium-sized company. As part of his job, he supports a young project manager, Robert, with less experience in the preparation of a restructuring project.

Michael Stone

Michael is 36 years old. He has just started his new job in the in-house consulting department at a medium-sized company. Previously, he was a manager and project leader at one of the MBB consultancies. He looks back on more than eight years of consulting experience and has completed more than 25 consulting projects during this time.

Robert Mayer

Robert is 28 years and is a Junior Project Manager in the in-house consulting department at the same company as Michael. He knows the company very well, as he has been working for that company for several years. Before he joined the in-house consulting department, he worked in accounting.

To support Robert in his new project, a restructuring situation in a subsidiary, Michael offers coaching on project-specific topics. He helps him with project management methods and procedures from management consulting. In this way, he supports Robert in preparing the project efficiently and helps him anticipate many of the risks that may arise during project implementation.

I hope you enjoy reading it.

PS. This is a fictional project, a fictional company, and fictional characters. All similarities are coincidental and all representations from the project are made up.

1. Define project goals and scope

Michael was sitting in the office alone. He usually sits in the office with three other colleagues from the in-house consulting department, but it seems that everyone else has meetings. The office is old and furnished with white furniture. Everyone has their workstation with a laptop, two additional monitors, and a filing cabinet under the desk. He was looking out the fifth-floor window and starting to daydream a bit when Robert came storming into the office, muttering something.

Robert was visibly upset and nervous. He was still mumbling something and clicking his mouse around frantically. "What a bummer," Michael heard him say, or "Where do I start?" or "They're giving me that!" Robert had just been promoted to junior project manager earlier that month. He had been in in-house consulting for two years as a consultant.

Michael walked over to Robert and asked, "Can I help you, Robert? Sounds like you are under a lot of stress?"

"Ah thank you Michael, but I don't think you can help me on this one. I am a freshly promoted project manager and what kind of project do I get to start with? A restructuring project of one of our subsidiaries! The constraints during Corona have taken a decent toll on the subsidiary, as they had mainly relied on brick-and-mortar retail in the past. Now many of the stores are to be closed, employees are to be laid off, and I get such a project as a junior project manager. Why doesn't an experienced project manager, who has done something like this before, get this kind of project?" Robert asked without directly addressing Michael.

"Okay, restructuring projects are never nice. But from my experience, I know that the project leaders of such topics can excel and recommend themselves for further positions along the ladder in the company. Moreover, restructuring projects follow a similar pattern: profitable vs. non-profitable units, number of hierarchical levels, distribution of employees among managers and executives also called "span of control", which activities can be automated and so on," Michael replied quietly.

Robert's eyes snapped open. "You have done a restructuring project before?" he asked.

"Yes, several times," Michael nodded. "I would be happy to help you with that."

"You are saving me!" Robert said, looking visibly relieved. "That would be great if you could help me with that. As laying people off is also an integral part of the project, I have a lot of respect for the project and do not want to do anything wrong. And to be honest, I currently do not know where to start."

"As with any project, we start with the project goals and scope. I like to use 'What is different after successful project completion?' as a guiding question to comprehensively define the project goals and scope. After all, the project goals define what the project should accomplish and what the results will be. It helps to define the objectives SMART[2] and to define the project deliverables in terms of deliverable types, for example, a concept," Michael said.

"Yes, exactly! Timo, our department head, just briefly threw the project over the fence to me and forwarded some emails. He did not say much about it because he caught this project assignment between two board meetings. He wants me to come up with an initial proposal on the project goals by Monday afternoon so we can discuss them. But without a proper briefing from Timo on the project, I do not think, that it is realistic," Robert said.

"Why? He forwarded you a lot of e-mails, you said. Surely you can formulate an initial proposal for the project goals, can't you?" Michael asked.

Robert hesitated. "But I need a proper briefing on the project," Robert replied.

"Certainly. But Timo only asked you for a first draft of the project goals. Besides, this way you can show him that the promotion to project manager was deserved if you prepare for the appointment accordingly," Michael said.

---

[2] Goal definition according to SMART: Specific, measurable, attractive, relevant, and time bound.

Robert nodded.

"Well, let's read the emails together and define a first draft of the project goals and scope. On Monday we can read this draft again and then you can take the results to Timo. Setup a meeting with him now, so he does not have to do it," Michael said, got his chair, and sat down next to Robert.

After Robert and Michael read through all the emails together, Michael continued, "In addition to the project goals, the project scope needs to be defined precisely to avoid delays later in the project. So:

- What are the project's goals, outcomes, and measures?
- What areas and topics are part of the project, and which are not part of the project?"

Michael took a pad and wrote down the two questions. "Even though the goals, outcomes, and measures sound similar at first glance, we need to differentiate:

1. Goals answer the question 'What do I want to accomplish?' or 'What has changed after the project is completed successfully?'
2. The answer to the question answers the next question 'What results do I need for this?'
3. The measures then define, who must do what by when to achieve the results.

In other words: 'What do you want to be different at the end of the project and what do you need to do in the project to achieve that?'"

Michael continued, "In terms of measures, it will become clearer whether specific areas, departments, or data are to be analyzed. And if so, who do we need for this in the project and the steering committee?"[3]

"Based on the objectives, deliverables, and measures, it is possible to define how much time and resources (budget and staff) the project will require. Therefore, within the project preparation and planning, it helps to conduct interviews with all steering committee participants to obtain

---

[3] Steering committee. this refers to a decision-making and escalation council that is superordinate to the project. It is composed of high-ranking representatives and stakeholders of the areas affected by the project.

their expectations on the project and to coordinate or catch deviations from the defined goals and project scope at an early stage," Michael continued.

Robert nodded, "Before the project kick-off, we need to have the goals reconciled by the steering committee so that the project team is officially mandated to conduct the project." (Also see Chapter 7).

"That's right!" Michael said. "The project goals and scope need to be written down. As part of the initial steering committee, these should be presented on one slide. This avoids ad hoc assignments and misunderstandings later in the project."

"But why do I have to specify what is not included in the project scope?" Robert asked curiously.

"Let's take the current restructuring project as an example: What are you supposed to analyze and restructure? Should only the branches and the branch network be restructured, or further departments within the subsidiary itself, i.e., the HR department, the accounting department, and the IT department? These are all important aspects that have an impact on the scope of the project and therefore influence the time, budget, and project staff required," Michael said.

"Oh," Robert said, and it clicked, "so that later in the steering committee no one can say they thought that was part of the project and misunderstandings are avoided early on."

"Exactly! We do not want any misunderstandings at the beginning to prevent early project delays or risks. I have an idea for exactly that slide that I can send you. Let me draw it on my laptop and I'll give you the slide later. Unless you have templates for something like this in the company already. Then you should use those, of course," Michael explained.

"Great. If you send me the slide, I'll be happy to use it. Timo has given me until Monday to define the project goals and scope. How would you proceed with that now?" Robert asked.

"Robert, what do you think, the goal of the project is?" Michael asked, grabbing a notebook.

"Currently the subsidiary has a slightly negative business result (EBIT[4]) and to become positive again, is the main goal" Robert replied. "In addition, there is a company requirement that we must achieve a 6%-EBIT-margin per company. Timo had already sent me the subsidiary's figures. Those were in one of the Excel documents we looked into."

Michael agreed by nodding: "Then a restructuring needs to be conducted to close the EBIT gap by implementing a catalog of measures to achieve the 6%-EBIT-margin. I would also define a safety buffer of 1-2% of the EBIT margin in the target. If Timo or the steering committee don't want the safety buffer, that's okay, but you proposed it as the project manager, so you are prepared."

"The next thing is to define the deliverables. If you have multiple subprojects, you need to define the outcomes per subproject, so the project team knows exactly what they need to achieve. Based on the deliverables, you can define the actions needed to achieve the outcome with the project team," Michael said.

Robert approved. "I can already calculate the EBIT gap in € in advance, so we have an absolute value, which according to a first estimate is around € 9 million," Robert added.

"I would define the absolute outcome for the project as an outcome of the project, even if you already have an approximate number in mind," Michael said.

"Would you see calculating the EBIT gap as part of the project? I could probably calculate that in half a day during work and already take it to Timo" Robert asked.

"Certainly, you could calculate it before the beginning of the project, but I would calculate it with the team in the project for two political reasons:

1. It will be the first official project result that the project can quickly show to the steering committee and further stakeholders.
2. The result will be agreed on in the project. Therefore, no stakeholder or member of the steering committee can ask

---

[4] Earnings Before Interest and Taxes: a company's profits in a particular period, before taking away interest charges and tax payments

'Where do these figures come from?' and they have a sense of contribution. In addition, I would always reconcile the figures with the accounting department of the subsidiary, to make sure, you have up-to-date numbers.

Nonetheless, you should have an approximate gap amount in mind to properly plan time, budget, and staff," Michael explained.

"That sounds good, and I will suggest it to Timo. If you send me your slide idea, I will define the project scope myself and then let you have a look on Monday, if that is okay with you?" Robert asked.

Michael started laughing and said, "Of course, we can look at it together on Monday. What are you going to call the project or is there already a name?" Michael asked.

Robert shrugged his shoulders. "I don't know, I haven't thought about that yet."

"How about Project 'Phoenix'? A restructuring can always be a bit tricky, so I recommend an alias, and in a restructuring project, Phoenix, like a phoenix from the ashes, fits well," Michael smiled.

Robert agreed, "Sounds good. I'll take it to Timo on Monday. I'll get the first draft done before the weekend."

Michael nodded and sat down at his laptop. He quickly created the slide in MS PowerPoint and sent it to Robert.

***

On Monday morning, Michael was the first one in the office. Like every Monday morning, he got himself a coffee and checked the intranet to see what was new in the company. Gradually, the rest of his colleagues came into the office and started working.

"Michael, do you have a moment for our topic?" Robert asked. When Michael nodded, Robert came to Michael with his laptop and showed him the following slides:

The company's goal of a 6% EBIT margin for the subsidiary ABC Ltd. is to be achieved

Problem

Negative business result at our subsidiary ABC Ltd.

Company's goal is a 6% EBIT-margin

Due to current developments, it is not assumed that the subsidiary will generate 6% EBIT-margin by itself

Goals of the project

Implement a restructuring project to close the EBIT gap by June 30th, 2024, at ABC Ltd.

Implement a catalog of measures to achieve the 6% EBIT-margin by June 30th, 2024

Implement further measures to achieve additional 1.5 percentage points EBIT margin by June 30th, 2024, as a safety buffer

Source: Project-Team Phoenix

Overall result of restructuring currently in coordination with Accounting - estimated at approx. €9 million

Overall result	Subproject	Results	Main measures
Approx. €9 million[1] in restructuring measures implemented by June 30th, 2024	PMO	EBIT gap for ABC Ltd. defined by 15.07.23 and distributed to subprojects	• Define and reconcile EBIT-gap with Accounting of ABC Ltd. (C. Grohe) • Allocate absolute EBIT-gap according to subprojects by 15.07.23 (C. Grohe) • Reconcile overall EBIT-gap in steering committee on 09.08.23 (R. Mayer) • …
	SP 1: Branch network	X million in restructuring measures implemented in the branch network by June 30th, 2024	• Conduct analysis of branch network by 31.07.23 (H. Wolters) • Define restructuring and efficiency measures by 07.10.23 (H. Wolters) • Reconcile restructuring and efficiency measures by 07.12.23 (M. Hinsch) • Implement restructuring and efficiency measures by 30.06.24 (departments) • …
	SP 2: E-commerce	X million in e-commerce restructuring measures implemented by June 30th, 2024	• Conduct analysis of e-commerce by 31.07.23 (T. Horn) • Define restructuring and efficiency measures by 07.10.23 (T. Horn) • Reconcile restructuring and efficiency measures by 07.12.23 (A. Schmid) • Implement restructuring and efficiency measures by 30.06.24 (departments) • …

Not in project scope

• Departments: Operations
• Overhead functions (HR, Marketing)

1 | Absolute EBIT-gap in reconciliation with Accounting department of ABC Ltd
Source: Project Team Phoenix

www.Consulting-University.com

Michael read through the contents and nodded. "As a first draft for discussion, I think it's good!" Michael said and looked at Robert.

"I'm not convinced yet, since the slides are all text," Robert said, leaning back in his chair.

"Sure, you could add icons here to make it more graphically appealing, but the slide is just the means to an end. It serves as the basis for a deep technical discussion and the subsequent documentation. We want to focus on what's important: the content. As this needs to be written down, agreed upon, and approved. For this purpose, your slide is well structured, and every participant of the steering committee knows the project goals and the project scope. Furthermore, everyone knows what is not part of the project. In this format, changes can also be quickly made during the steering committee meeting, so that these can also be agreed upon and approved immediately," Michael replied and continued:

"In the second step, I would always create a profile for each subproject and send it to the subproject managers for coordination and reconciliation. As a project manager, I advise you to fill it out yourself initially, as far as this is possible. Otherwise, you will get something back but never what you asked for. Many do not see the added value in it and then fill it out while doing something else or not paying attention to details. You have already filled out the essential measures and milestones.[5] Therefore, create a first draft yourself, mark it as such, and ask the subproject leaders for adjustments and additions. Offer the subproject managers to make the adjustments in a joint meeting. This way you can moderate the process and respond directly to questions. Also, point out to them that these slides will be reconciled by the steering committee. Sure, this is another formal act of reconciliation, but this way you'll make sure the whole project team has the same ideas." Michael showed Robert the following slide as a scribble[6], which is still blank:

---

[5] Initially, it will not always be possible to name the essential measures and milestones with times and responsibilities. This must be supplemented by the whole project team during the project preparations and planning meetings.

[6] A "scribble" is usually a handwritten draft of a slide that represents the structure and initial input. Slide structures can be quickly reconciled and adjusted using scribbles. For readability reasons, this "scribble" has already been created in Microsoft PowerPoint.

Project profile - Project Phoenix
Subproject 1: Branch network

Subproject	Responsible	Start date	End date	Budget	Project employees
Branch network	Name (OU)	dd.mm.yyyy	dd.mm.yyyy	x.x million €	X FTE

Problem
- Lorem Ipsum

Goal
- Lorem Ipsum

Potential risks
- Lorem Ipsum

Required input
- Lorem Ipsum

Results/ Output/ Deliverables
- Lorem Ipsum

Project Team
- Name (OU), capacity
- …

Measures and associated milestones (date and person responsible)
- Measure 1 (dd.mm.yyyy, N.N. (OU))
- Measure 2 (dd.mm.yyyy, Maike Hinsch (OU))
- …

"You're right about that. I will prepare them and send them to the project team after the meeting with Timo," Robert replied. "In addition, I calculated the EBIT gap on Friday to get a rough idea, of how big the project will be. The EBIT gap is around €9 million."

Michael nodded. "That's not a small amount, but it's doable. When are you presenting this to Timo today?"

"He accepted my appointment at 1:00 pm. I'll know more after that," Robert replied. He picked up his laptop and went back to his seat.

———

Learning Nuggets

o   Define project goals and scope using the SMART method, to be as specific as possible: "Who does what by when?", is the question, which must be answered.

o   Define what is not included in the project scope to provide clarity early in the project as to what is and what is not part of the project.

o   Write down the project goals and scope in a structured way so that a project outsider can quickly grasp and understand the content. It is best to use the format that is used in your company to avoid additional work.

o   If necessary, conduct interviews with all important steering committee participants, department heads, and stakeholders beforehand so that everyone has a common understanding of the project. For this purpose, the project goals, project scope, and project organization (see Chapter 5) should already be defined as a draft. In addition, the interviews can be used to request resources from the department heads.

o   Define the first measures for the subprojects and fill out the project profile yourself, as far as possible. At first glance, this may seem like more work for you, but it will cost you much less coordination and reconciliation time as a project manager.

———

Checklist

o   Project objectives and scope (deliverables and measures) are defined.
o   It is defined as what is not included in the project scope.
o   If needed: Interviews were conducted with all steering committee participants and relevant stakeholders regarding project goals and scope.
o   Project goals and scope are agreed upon with steering committee participants before the first steering committee.

2. Determine the project sponsor

Robert came into the office after his appointment with Timo. He was beaming with joy and gave Michael a thumbs up. After he put his laptop down into the docking station, he went to Michael. "Timo thought it was great!" he said, beaming all over his face." In particular, he thought the aspect of what's not included in the project scope was very well laid out and structured."

"I'm glad, that I could help you, Robert. Did you also get more information about the project?" Michael asked, leaning back in his chair.

"Yes, the instruction to conduct a restructuring project comes directly from Dr. Haupt, our CFO. The managing director of the subsidiary "ABC Ltd.", Ms. Simoneit, is of course not enthusiastic but informed. She will inform her relevant department heads and we will set up a mixed project team of our in-house consulting department and the subsidiary," Robert said.

"That sounds good. Then you'll have your project sponsor too, if the CFO, Dr. Haupt, brought the project up," Michael said.

Robert screwed up his face. "What do you mean? I didn't want to involve Dr. Haupt any further in the project. He gets a monthly report on the project's progress, and then Timo and I sit in the steering committee, as well as Ms. Simoneit and a few of her department heads."

Now Michael screwed up his face. "Robert, this is a restructuring project in which personnel measures are planned too. Who decides in the steering committee if Timo and Ms. Simoneit cannot agree on who must be laid off for example?" Michael asked, shaking his head.

Robert paused and took a deep breath. "I hadn't thought of it that way, to be honest. I thought we didn't need to involve Dr. Haupt any further," Robert said, looking at Michael.

Michael leaned forward to him: "The essential aspect of a sufficiently high sponsor is that the project has an advocate and supporter. After all, this project involves drastic changes for the entire workforce of ABC Ltd., which not everyone will like. A restructuring project needs sufficient support from C-Level executives if there are risks or different opinions within the project. After all, it's about drastic changes that must be decided within the steering committee," Michael said very calmly.

Robert nodded.

"Look, Robert, in addition to the role of advocate and supporter, the project sponsor[7] must take on other roles as well. For example:

- Provides funding for the project and releases the project budget.
- Serves as the ultimate escalation authority in the project for issues, risks, and challenges.
- Issues and withdraws the project from external service providers (when involved).
- Ensures that project objectives are consistent with the company's strategic direction.
- Communicates project goals and scope and his/her expectations to the entire project team.
- Makes decisions in the steering committee and supports the project in the operational implementation of the decisions made.
- Helps the project identify appropriate committees, if necessary, when the steering committee is unable or unwilling to make the decisions.

To meet these requirements, he or she must be at least a department head, if not a division head:

- The more units affected by the project, the higher up the hierarchy the project sponsor must be within the line organization.
- He or she must be at least one hierarchical level above the affected managers and departments.

For larger projects and when more departments are affected or involved, the management or a board member should be the project sponsor, as is the case with us. In addition, two project sponsors are often named in

---

[7] The project sponsor can be seen as a client or customer, as the project sponsor provides funding and acts as the final decision and escalation authority within the project.

many projects to ensure assertiveness in all affected areas and departments within the companies.

If no decisions are made during the project, this is usually due to weak staffing of the project steering committee and, above all, the project sponsor. As a result, this leads to delays in the project and could even lead to project termination. The core question is therefore which sponsors the project needs before it starts to be successfully implemented and enforced," Michael explained.

"You're right," Robert said, "This restructuring project will involve a lot of changes in the subsidiary. It only makes sense for Dr. Haupt to be on the steering committee as CFO and support the decisions made. But what is the best way to approach Dr. Haupt and tell him he's appointed to be the project sponsor?"

"To be honest, I suspect that Dr. Haupt already knows that. After all, he commissioned the restructuring project and wants to be involved in the decision-making process. Therefore, I would speak with Timo and put Dr. Haupt into the project organization (see Chapter 5) and provide him with the project outline[8] later via Timo. That way, he can still make changes if he doesn't see himself as a project sponsor," Michael replied.

———

Learning Nuggets

- The project sponsor is an advocate and supporter of the project when it comes to changes that not all participants want to support. Thus, the project sponsor is a central figure in the project, he will not be directly involved operationally. Nevertheless, he is the central figure for decision-making and acts as an escalation option.
- The more departments or people are affected by the project, the higher the project sponsor must be in terms of hierarchy within the line organization.

---

[8] The project outline summarizes the project in total. This is a short presentation: goals, objectives, project scope, project organization, project profiles, etc. Before the first steering committee, the project outline should therefore be reconciled with the project sponsor (and all steering committee participants), for example within the interviews, so that they can all intervene and correct it if necessary, before the project begins.

- o The project sponsor must be at least one hierarchical level above the managers affected by the project to be able to enforce and implement decisions.
- o If necessary, the project requires two project sponsors if several departments or divisions are affected by the project to enforce the decisions operationally.

———

Checklist

- o The project sponsor has been named and has agreed to be the project sponsor.[9]
- o Actual organizational charts of participating departments and companies can help you if you do not know, who will be participating in the project.

---

[9] Often, the project sponsor places the order or releases the project budget, so that the project sponsor is implicitly determined.

3. Identify and analyze relevant stakeholders

"Besides the project sponsor, have you looked at the other stakeholders[10] that the project will affect?" Michael asked when Robert had settled back into his seat. "I suspect that many people and a wide variety of stakeholders will be affected by the project," Michael added as Robert looked over at him.

"I always do a stakeholder analysis at the beginning of the project during the analysis phase," Robert replied.

"But a stakeholder analysis should always be done before the project starts. Especially in restructuring projects, there are many affected employees, managers, and even external groups," Michael said and stood up.

Robert looked at Michael questioningly.

"Every project affects the interests of others. In most cases, these are the employees and managers who are also involved in the project. However, the project can also affect the interests of other stakeholders, such as the works council, the public, or investors. In restructuring projects in particular, many stakeholders are affected: Employees, managers, the works council, supervisory board, other committees, and even the public or press if there will be a large lay-off," Michael explained.

"Yes, I'm aware of that. But I should be fine to conduct a stakeholder analysis in the analysis phase at the beginning of the project. Why should I have to deal with this now?" Robert asked.

"Quite simple, if the affected stakeholders are not considered and, if necessary, integrated into the project at an early stage, this can lead to project delays or even project termination right at the start. Therefore, all stakeholders should be defined and analyzed before the project starts:

---

[10] Stakeholders and stakeholder groups: These are all people, committees, departments that will be affected by the project or for whom the project is of interest. This can involve investors, the press, the government, or the public too.

- Which stakeholders are directly affected by the project? (Within the project itself, within the company, and outside of the company.)
- What is the expected attitude of the stakeholders towards the project? Do they support or oppose the project?
- What influence do these stakeholders have on the project? Can they intervene or even stop the project?
- What is the expected behavior of the stakeholders and what are the consequences for the project?

Only this kind of stakeholder analysis can show, where there is a need for information and action before, during, and after the project. During the project, this has a particular influence on the communication strategy and change management. After all, you always need a communication strategy and change management in a restructuring project. Otherwise, you can very quickly do a lot of damage with the project, which can have a long-term impact on your company," Michael explained further.

"Maybe you're right Michael," Robert said and continued, "I'll create a draft that I can reconcile with Timo."

"Don't forget the supervisory board as a stakeholder. I suspect that the supervisory board has commissioned Dr. Haupt with the restructuring project or that Dr. Haupt got the "go" from them. Either way, the supervisory board will be regularly informed about the progress of the project. This will mean additional reporting work for you as a project manager," Michael said.

"The stakeholder analysis can be performed using a simple spreadsheet template. Here, assumptions and hypotheses are made, which should be discussed within the project team. In particular, the consequences for the project can be presented by many possible options. This should be coordinated with the project sponsor depending on the stakeholder. From my experience, it is advisable to involve the works council from the very beginning in a restructuring project to avoid delays," Michael explained.

***

The day was coming to an end and Michael was starting to clean up his workstation when Robert showed up with his laptop. "Michael, do you have a few more minutes to look at my stakeholder slides? I've done some stakeholder analysis already and just wanted to know from you if I am doing it right. Then I can still do the further analyses and take the slides with me to Timo in the next meeting," Robert asked.

"Sure thing! Show me what you've got," Michael said and cleared his desk so that Robert could put his laptop down.

Stakeholder analysis

No.	Stakeholder	Project support	Influence on the project	Expected behavior	Consequences for the project
1.	Works council	Unlikely, as restructuring and HR measures are to be expected.	Initially low. Coordination of measures necessary before implementation.	As soon as the works council hears about the project, we will have to provide regular information on planned measures.	Option 1) Inform works council in advance and convince them of the necessity of the restructuring measures. Option 2) Keep project secret and then present measures to the works council when final.
2.	Staff of the subsidiary ABC Ltd. (employees and managers)	Unlikely, as restructuring and HR measures are to be expected.	Minor, but could inform works council.	Inform works council or the public (press) about the measures.	Introduction of comprehensive communication strategy and change management as a project component.
3.	...				

"So far, I have only analyzed the works council and the workforce, i.e., all employees and managers of the subsidiary. But I have identified the following stakeholders that I still need to analyze:

- supervisory board,
- public and press,
- other committees within the company,
- the workforce of our parent company."

Michael nodded. "That looks good, doesn't it? You've done a good job of representing the subsidiary's works council and workforce. I agree with the 'consequences for the project'. With the works council, we do have two options and within the project organization you need a communication strategy including change management," Michael said.

He continued, "You now see why it makes sense to do a stakeholder analysis before the project starts?" Michael asked.

"I probably would have planned a change management as well, but I don't know if I would have come up with a complete communications strategy on my own. Since this project will affect many stakeholders, this is an important point that I would have noticed too late, if necessary," Robert said and nodded.

Learning Nuggets

- The stakeholder analysis must be conducted with the project team before the project begins.
- In particular, the possible consequences for the project must be considered in all further project preparation and project work.
- Corporate committees can be stakeholders too, if the decisions made in the project must be supported or decided by this committee. This is particularly important for very large companies and groups, who have such committees to prepare decisions on C-Level.

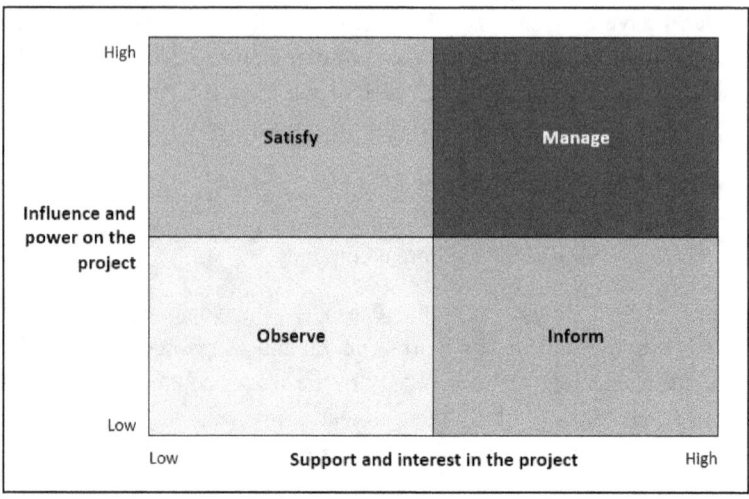

Stakeholder-Analysis chart to classify all relevant stakeholders.

———

Checklist

o   Stakeholder analysis is conducted within the project team before the start of the project.

o   Stakeholder analysis is discussed with trustful colleagues, who can assess if there are any more stakeholders or consequences for the project.

o   Consequences and implications from the stakeholder analysis are applied and considered in further project preparation and work.

4. Define and coordinate project resources

When Michael came into the office the next morning, Robert was already sitting at his laptop and typing diligently. He made a very concentrated impression but reacted immediately when Michael came in. "Good morning, Michael," he said.

"Good morning, Robert. Busy with your project preparation again?" Michael asked curiously.

"Yes, I am currently planning the project resources, i.e., budget and staff," Robert replied.

"Project resources?" Michael had to smile, "Are we allowed to call our employees a resource here? I am asking because I got really into some trouble once with a client, for calling his employees resources."

"Alright, you're right about that. But under resources, we summarize the factors that are necessary for the implementation of the project. This includes budget and internal staff, but also external service providers like consultants. In addition to a sufficient project budget, the project staff with the right skills and experience from the various departments must be planned for the project," Robert said.

"It's good that you plan this before the project even starts. Without enough budget and the right people committed before the project starts, the project doesn't need to start," Michael said.

Robert nodded, "I'm curious to see whom we get from the subsidiary as team members. I'm allowed to schedule two consultants from our in-house consulting department, but we'll see whom we get from the subsidiary to see how seriously they take the project. I am not implying anything about the colleagues, but so far, the quality of the temporarily provided project members from the line has always been very different. Depending on how important the departments take the project, the better the colleagues are provided," Robert explained.

Meanwhile, Michael sat down at his desk and flipped his laptop open. "That's just normal. What do you think I've experienced in my years as a management consultant? We always had it contractually guaranteed that the client would provide experts from the company if it was necessary. I mean, the worse the employees and experts are, the longer they take and the worse the project results will be. Many companies underestimate the impact a good project manager on the client side can have on the project outcome. Good feedback on ideas or concepts alone causes a better exchange between the employees and the consultants than if the project manager only complains about spelling mistakes or goes on about the line thickness of graphs in PowerPoint presentations."

"What, the line thickness of graphs?" Robert laughed.

"Yes, we had sent our presentation to the project manager from the client for the steering committee and all that came back was the note: "Content good, please change the line thickness to 0.75 PT for the graphs by 10 am tomorrow." That was 11 pm when we received that email. You can imagine how our motivation was when we changed the line thickness by midnight," Michael laughed.

Robert shook his head. "I have made the experience too, that the more complex the project becomes, the more experienced and recognized in the company the project manager has to be, but also the project staff, to achieve very good results. Fortunately, in-house consulting enjoys a good reputation, which has opened many doors for us so far," Robert explained.

"Do we need written confirmation or approval of the project budget from the Accounting department at the company?" Michael asked.

"What do you mean?" Robert asked.

"I always book my hours to a project number. Does the internal project staff do that too? Do we need such a project number and a budget for them? Or how is that handled here in the company?" Michael asked.

"Oh, that. No. I would only seek written approval from Accounting and Timo if you are asking for an external budget. If we want to hire an external management consultancy, we need approval from Timo and Accounting. Then we get a project number and can check the invoices from the consultancy. But it's not relevant for internal projects," Robert explained.

"Okay, good to know, and how do you do that with scheduled employees from other departments or even the subsidiaries? What has worked here in the company to get the person or the committed capacity?" Michael asked.

"Once the people have been identified, I have their disciplinary managers send me a written commitment by e-mail. The manager then states the project, the project staff, and the assured capacity over the respective project period. As the project manager, I can then refer to this e-mail if any problems occur. Ideally, we agree on fixed project days too and, if necessary, work in one specific project room, so that the employees can really collaborate on the project and we have everyone together in one room," Robert explained.

"That's exactly how I would do it and also have the project resources reconciled in the steering committee. Even though the reality is often different, I advocate assured project capacities of at least 60% per person, so that the project has priority over line activities. Unfortunately, my experience has shown me that despite capacity assurances, the reality is often different. Despite the assured 60%, the employee only works 30% on the project. As a result, the employee does less project work, the project goals are not met or the quality of work in the project is poor. Often the employee suffers the most because the project on one side and the line activities on the other tear him apart," Michael said. [11]

"You're right. But then it's our job as project managers to take countermeasures as quickly as possible and to talk to the disciplinary manager and demand the agreed capacity. If necessary, this must be escalated to the steering committee if there is no common understanding on behalf of the manager," Robert said.

Michael looked at him. "You're right, and to anticipate exactly that, I use an overview of all the project staff in the steering committee, including percentages of capacity allocated to the project. That is to achieve awareness among all steering committee participants on the one side and to have these agreed-upon capacities documented in the meeting's

---

[11] Why does this often fail? While on a project, the employee can no longer do 100% of his "normal" line activities, so that activities must be postponed or done by someone else. The employee must therefore be enabled to work on the project as well.

minutes. If project members have not been named (N. N.) yet this must be documented with the project capacity for reasons of transparency too. At least, this has always worked well in the past for me. That's how we always had our capacities secured," Michael laughed. "I have an idea of how you can present that on a slide. I'll quickly scribble the slide and then give it to you," Michael said.

"Very good. Just give me the slide and I'll create it then. I'll be happy to show it to you and maybe you'll have some feedback on how I can make it look better," Robert said happily.

Michael gave him the slide and Robert began to create it. When he was done, he took his laptop and sat down next to Michael.

Project capacities

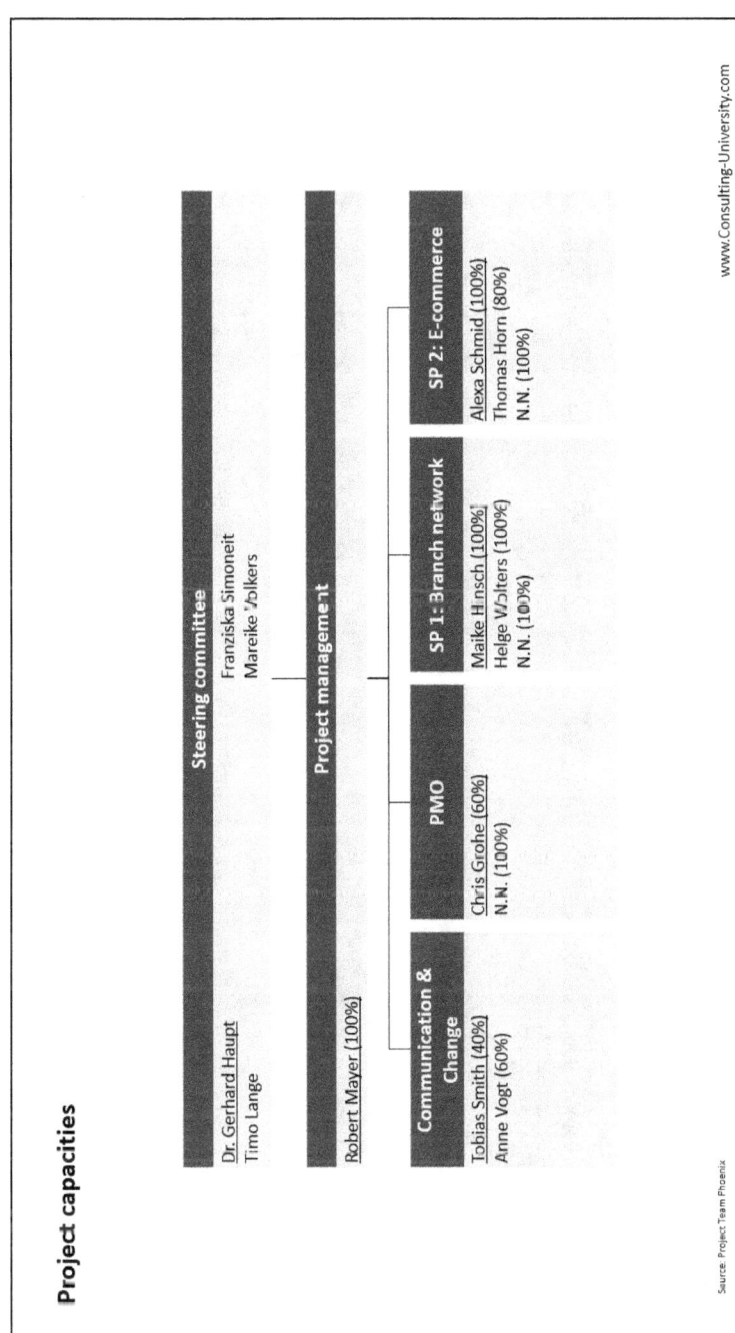

Steering committee

Dr. Gerhard Haupt
Timo Lange

Franziska Simoneit
Mareike Volkers

Project management

Robert Mayer (100%)

Communication & Change

Tobias Smith (40%)
Anne Vogt (60%)

PMO

Chris Grohe (60%)
N.N. (100%)

SP 1: Branch network

Maike Hinsch (100%)
Helge Walters (100%)
N.N. (100%)

SP 2: E-commerce

Alexa Schmid (100%)
Thomas Horn (80%)
N.N. (100%)

Source: Project Team Phoenix

www.Consulting-University.com

Project organization

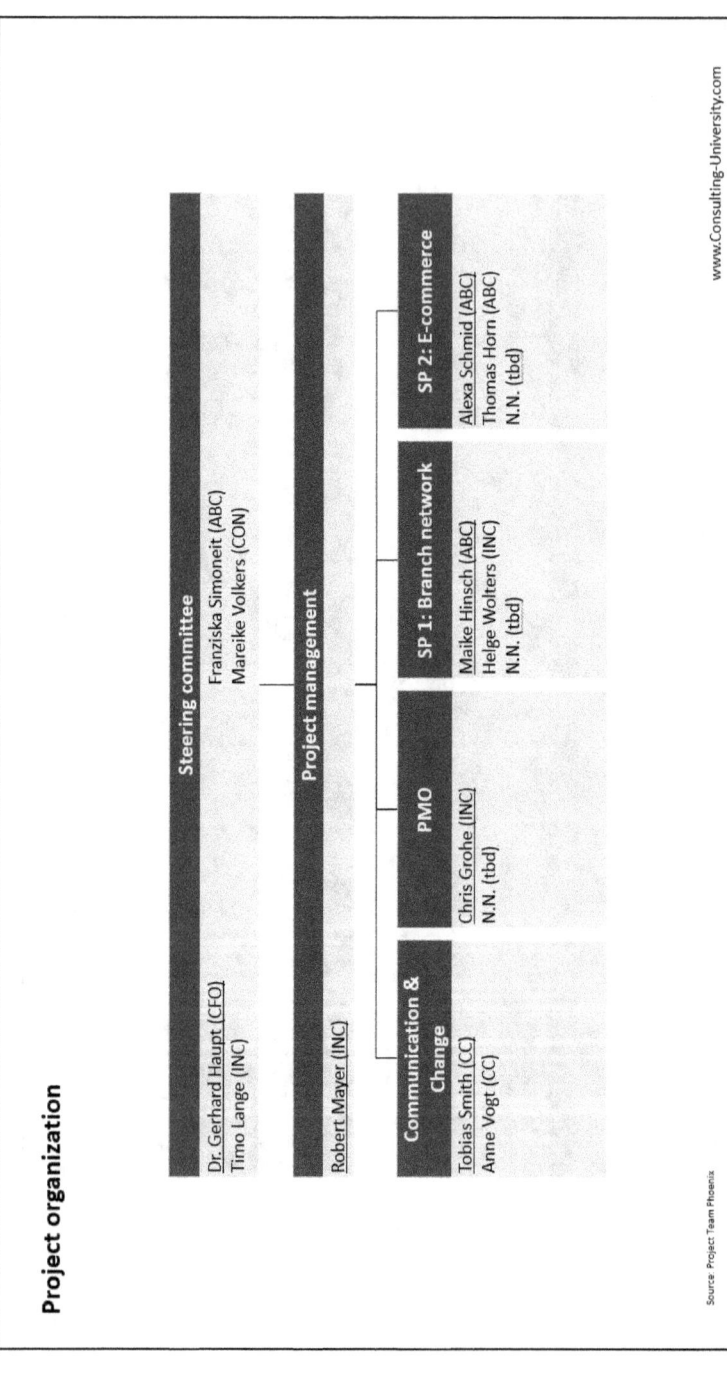

Steering committee

Dr. Gerhard Haupt (CFO)
Timo Lange (INC)

Franziska Simoneit (ABC)
Mareike Volkers (CON)

Project management

Robert Mayer (INC)

Communication & Change	PMO	SP 1: Branch network	SP 2: E-commerce
Tobias Smith (CC)	Chris Grohe (INC)	Maike Hinsch (ABC)	Alexa Schmid (ABC)
Anne Vogt (CC)	N.N. (tbd)	Helge Wolters (INC)	Thomas Horn (ABC)
		N.N. (tbd)	N.N. (tbd)

"I think it's good that you've put the project team members into an organizational chart. Everyone can see immediately how much capacity is available or necessary for each subproject. In addition, you can use the same slide for the project organization by replacing the capacity information in % by their departments. Steering committee members can see who is located where," Michael said.

"Have you already made a reservation for a project room for the duration of the project? I think it's good if the project team members have a central point of contact. In addition, there will probably be a lot of interviews, so it may make sense to reserve a separate meeting room for the project as well so that interviews and meetings can always take place in the same room," Michael explained.

"I'm already on that, although I've been told that I'll probably only get one large room. That will have to do then," Robert replied.

―――

Learning Nuggets

- Project resources include budgets, rooms, external project staff, and of course the internal project staff that is relevant for the implementation of the project. Do not underestimate the necessary budgets for IT and software and consult experts from your company to estimate them when necessary.
- Depending on the company structure, the project start may require approval and, for example, further approval from the accounting department if the budget is required.
- A written assurance (by e-mail) of the project staff's capacity from their managers and supervisors makes escalation possible. This can occur when the project staff member does not contribute to the project in their capacity or with poor quality.
- Ideally, fixed project days are defined so that project members can exchange ideas and plan better, besides their line organization activities and duties.
- If it is apparent at the planning stage of the project, that too little relevant expertise or capacity is available in the company for the

project, the use of external consultants and the corresponding provision of the budget must be discussed.

———

Checklist

- o All project members have been appointed and informed accordingly about the project and their tasks.
- o Written assurance (for example, via e-mail) was obtained from the managers and supervisors for the project staff (project, name of employee, capacity, duration).
- o Budgets were requested and released as needed from the required departments.
- o If needed, a project room and additional meeting rooms were reserved for the duration of the project.
- o If necessary, the project was approved by the relevant departments (if necessary, this also happens only in the steering committee kick-off (see Chapter 7)).

5. Determine the project organization

Michael had received his first real assignments and was analyzing the various online business models of direct competitors to identify quick wins for his own company when Robert suddenly stood in front of his desk.

"Do you have time for me later?" Robert asked.

"Sure, what's up?" Michael asked curiously.

"I will work out the project organization and would like your feedback on that," Robert said.

"Yes, send me your draft, and as soon as I've looked over it, I'll get back to you! When do you need it by?" Michael asked.

"I'm supposed to send this to Timo by tomorrow night. I would send you a first draft this afternoon and if you could give me feedback by tomorrow morning, 10 am? Then I can incorporate your feedback," Robert said.

"Suggestion: send it to me today, you'll get my comments today, and tomorrow at nine we'll sit down and discuss my feedback?" Michael suggested.

"Thanks, Michael! We'll do that. I will set us up an appointment for tomorrow at nine o'clock," Robert replied.

***

In the afternoon, Michael received the slides on the project organization from Robert. He added his feedback and added a few new slide ideas that had proven successful in other projects. Then he sent the feedback to Robert as discussed, so they could discuss it together the next day.

***

At 08.45 Michael came into the office and sees that Robert is already sitting at his laptop. "Well, are you looking at my feedback right now?" Michael asked.

"Yes, you changed and noted a lot," Robert said, looking up from the laptop at Michael.

"It wasn't a lot of feedback. I sent along some slide ideas, so you'd have it in the right format straight away and not have to duplicate everything," Michael said, putting his bag down.

"Yes, I'm already transferring the slides so we can look at them together in a moment. If you get yourself a coffee, I'll be done in a minute," Robert said.

When Michael came back into the office with a coffee, Robert was already grinning at him. Michael put his coffee down on Robert's desk and rolled his office chair over to Robert so that they could both look at his monitor together.

"Maybe a couple of points up front, because you said I had quite a bit of feedback," Michael said, continuing, "The project organization provides guidelines and standards so that efficiency can be increased in the operational project work. I'm a friend of making the project organization a little more detailed and formalized rather than having questions come up later that bother you as a project manager."

Robert nodded and said, "I agree and found your points very helpful as well. Let's go through it. For me, the project organization includes the operational work in the project, i.e., committees, project roles & responsibilities, standards & framework in the project, appointments with the project team, and the project plan."

"Exactly! If the project organization works, it helps to anticipate delays and quality problems within the project. In addition, defined roles, responsibilities, and standards ensure efficiency in the project, as many adjustments and reconciliations are avoided. All aspects must be defined before the project starts and addressed at the project kick-off," Michael added.

"Shall we start with the project roles & responsibilities?" Robert asked, showing the following slide:

Project Roles & Responsibilities

Roll	Project Manager	PMO	Communication & Change (C&C)	Subproject Manager	Project staff
Person	Robert Mayer (INC)	Chris Grohe (INC)	Tobias Smith (CC)	Maike Hinsch (ABC) Alexa Schmid (ABC)	According to project organization
Tasks	▪ Manage, plan, and conduct the project ▪ Contact person for the steering committee ▪ Coach the subproject managers	▪ Conduct project reporting ▪ Follow-up on project risks ▪ Conduct steering committee (incl. preparation and follow-up)	▪ Plan and implement communication and change measures ▪ Sparring of the project management regarding C&C	▪ Coach the project staff ▪ Give feedback on concepts and analysis ▪ Inform steering committee about subprojects	▪ Conduct project work (analysis, concepts) ▪ Conduct workshops and interviews ▪ Reconcile work results
Responsibility	▪ Comply with project goals ▪ Make project decisions within the scope of the project ▪ Manage project risks ▪ Overall project responsibility	▪ Escalate decisions and risks to the project manager ▪ Monitor project plan ▪ Monitor project budget	▪ Responsible for the communication strategy and change measures	▪ Responsible for the subprojects ▪ Make subproject decisions within the scope of the subproject ▪ Monitor subproject goals	▪ Deep understanding of analysis and concepts ▪ Reconcile concepts

Source: Project Team Phoenix

"Exactly. The project roles result for the most part from the roles that are provided for in the project resources or project organization. You still had the steering committee listed here, but I would put that on a separate slide for "committees." That makes it clearer and separates it more clearly," Michael said.

"Do we need to list the project sponsor, steering committee participants, or experts we need?" asked Robert.

"The project sponsor should know their role, yet for special projects, it may make sense to document and communicate your expectations of the project sponsor. The steering committee participants are seen as a committee, which is why I would list the steering committee on a separate slide. If you can name the experts now or their tasks, they can be listed. But I don't see any added value if you just write: 'Expert - input provider if needed' on the slide. Or what do you think?" Michael asked.

"I like the idea of presenting the steering committee on a separate slide. I also agree with you about the other points. Then let's go directly to the slide for committees since we are already talking about it," Robert said.

Committees & Responsibilities

Board	Steering committee	Works council meeting
Responsible	Robert Mayer (INC)	Franziska Simoneit (ABC)
Tasks	▪ Report to the steering committee ▪ Prepare decisions and options for decision ▪ Present project status and subproject contents ▪ Coordinate necessary measures	▪ Prepare slides and content for the works council ▪ Conduct (preliminary) communication with the works council ▪ Negotiate with the works council on decided measures
Participants	▪ Defined steering committee members ▪ Project management incl. subproject managers	▪ Franziska Simoneit (ABC) ▪ Timo Lange (INC) ▪ Robert Mayer (INC) ▪ Delegated members of the works council
Goal/ Decision-making powers	▪ Make necessary project decisions ▪ Distribute necessary work orders within the project framework ▪ Escalate if required ▪ Coordinate measures for presentation to the works council	▪ Negotiate and coordinate measures with the works council

Robert put the slide down and asked, "What exactly do we need this slide for? I had already listed the steering committee in the rule meetings. I do not see the added value."

"Will you, as the project manager, lead the negotiations with the works council or will Ms. Simoneit, as the subsidiary's managing director, do it?" Michael asked.

"I will prepare many slides for this with the project team, but currently I assume that Ms. Simoneit will lead the negotiations," Robert replied.

"Exactly. Certainly, that is implicitly clear to many. Nevertheless, this slide brings transparency to the bodies in which the project will occur and who is responsible for its preparation and implementation. As soon as this slide has been shown and documented in the first steering committee, Ms. Simoneit can no longer plead that she did not know that she was responsible for the works council negotiations. Especially in the case of further committees outside the project sphere, it is important to determine who is responsible for preparing the content and who represents the project in the committee to the outside world. Otherwise, things can quickly get hectic if no reasonable documentation is available shortly before the works council meeting. Even if you or you as the project team prepare these slides, Ms. Simoneit has the responsibility for these slides in front of the works council and not you," Michael explained.

"So, this slide is primarily to clarify the responsibilities, the participants, and the associated tasks that the responsible party needs to take on," Robert said.

"Exactly! All the bodies that the project needs to enforce decisions in the organization must be listed here. In smaller projects, the project steering committee is sufficient. In larger projects and corporate organizations, the project steering committee decides, but it must later be approved by another committee before it can be implemented. Therefore, define which decisions in the project must be made in which committee. Take this into account in the project plan as well, since large company-wide committees are bound to certain deadlines and cycles[12] . This brings transparency to

---

[12] For example, board meetings often take place monthly and have a lead time of two to six weeks. Beforehand, it must be clarified what content will be presented and who is responsible for it.

the project if decisions are necessary. Here we connect project committees on the one hand and existing committees in the company on the other, in which the project with its contents and decisions must go in. If you have done a good stakeholder analysis, you will have had some committees in there too," Michael said.

"Next, I have a slide with appointments and meetings for the project team, which also lists the steering committees. You didn't have any comments here?", Robert asked and showed the slide.

Meetings within the project

Name	Daily	Weekly results presentation	Steering committee
Date & Duration	• Mondays, 10.00 - 10.30 • Tues. - Fri. , 09.00 - 09.30	• Thursdays, 15.00 - 16.00	• According to appointment • Every 8 weeks
Participant	• Project Manager • Subproject Manager • PMO • Project staff	• Project Manager • Subproject Manager • PMO • C&C	• Steering committee participants • Project Manager • Subproject Manager • PMO Leader • Manager C&C
Location	• Project room no. 312 • Additionally, MS Teams (Remote)	• Meeting room no. 543 • Additionally, MS Teams (Remote)	• Meeting room, tbd • Additionally, MS Teams (Remote)
Goal	• Coordinate operational work, next steps and risks	• Reconcile weekly results • Reconcile project reporting	• Get necessary decisions for project
Agenda	• Show project progress • Show planned activities • Highlight current risks/obstacles • Reconcile necessary decisions	• Present subproject using PMO templates • Monitor risks and next steps	• Management Summary & Status Quo • Deep Dive Subprojects • Identify risks and options • Make decisions

Source: Project Team Phoenix

www.Consulting-University.com

"Yes exactly, I have only added "Additionally MS Teams (Remote)" for the location, so that the project members can better plan further appointments. The important thing is to be present at the appointments, whether that is remote or on-site doesn't matter for now.

But I also think it's good that you include the subproject managers in the steering committee. Even though this is your responsibility, the responsibility for implementation lies with the subsidiary, and you have no disciplinary control over it. If they don't deliver the promised results on time, the subproject managers can explain this to the steering committee. I would also have them present their subproject results to the steering committee themselves. By doing this, the subproject managers will have the motivation to get good project results," Michael said.

"Depending on the size of the project, you also need a regular meeting with all (sub-)project managers to agree on risks, decisions, dependencies, and the status quo. With more than four subprojects I highly recommend this meeting type, which is why it is not necessary here. Instead of presenting the weekly results, it may also be necessary for large projects and programs to hold a PMO-Jour Fixe meeting[13] with the PMO and the project manager to sift through all the results," Michael added.

Robert nodded. "The next slide also came from you, Michael. I think it's good but does this one belongs on the first steering committee?" he asked, putting the slide down.

---

[13] The regular deadlines required for the project depend heavily on the size of the project. However, the following aspects must be clearly defined: date & duration; fixed participants, so that there is no wild forwarding and substitution; fixed objectives and recurring agenda, so that the participants prepare themselves for the dates. See appendix for more suggested dates including objectives and agenda.

Working mode & project rules

Working mode

- Core team works in project room no. 312
- Every morning "Daily" in the project room for all project members. Each subproject manager presents his subproject verbally:
  - Progress,
  - Planned Activities,
  - Risks,
  - Necessary decisions.
- Fridays remote/home office possible
- Tools in the project
  - Data storage: MS SharePoint (www.project/client.com)
  - Communication: MS Teams
  - Kanban board: Trello
  - Workshop tool: Mural.co
  - Templates on MS SharePoint

Project rules

- Prioritize the project over your line activity
- Deliver promised results in time and quality
- Indicate project risks early during the Daily (incl. countermeasures)
- **"Clean Desk Policy"** in the project room
- Use the provided templates and standards (see admin folder on SharePoint).
- **Be aware: This project is secret and in stealth mode,** as it is a restructuring project

Source: Project Team Phoenix

"No, it's purely for the project organization, so you can define standards on how to work in the project. This slide clarifies many issues before they arise in the project and promotes efficiency and transparency. In particular, standards for documents and documentation that are defined at the beginning avoid extensive adjustments when the concepts are merged later.

It also serves as a 'cover my a**' slide for you as the project manager. Define this slide at the beginning of the project and show it later at the project kick-off. This serves as the documentation that you have pointed out a "Clean Desk Policy" for example. In addition, this project will be secret, so you will also have it documented that you have pointed it out. Sure, this doesn't apply to all projects, but 'better safe than sorry' is what we used to say back then," Michael explained.

"I like that! There are so many aspects noted here that come up in every project and are clarified for everyone in the beginning.

Finally, the project plan, where you only put in the vacation times," Robert said, showing the last slide.

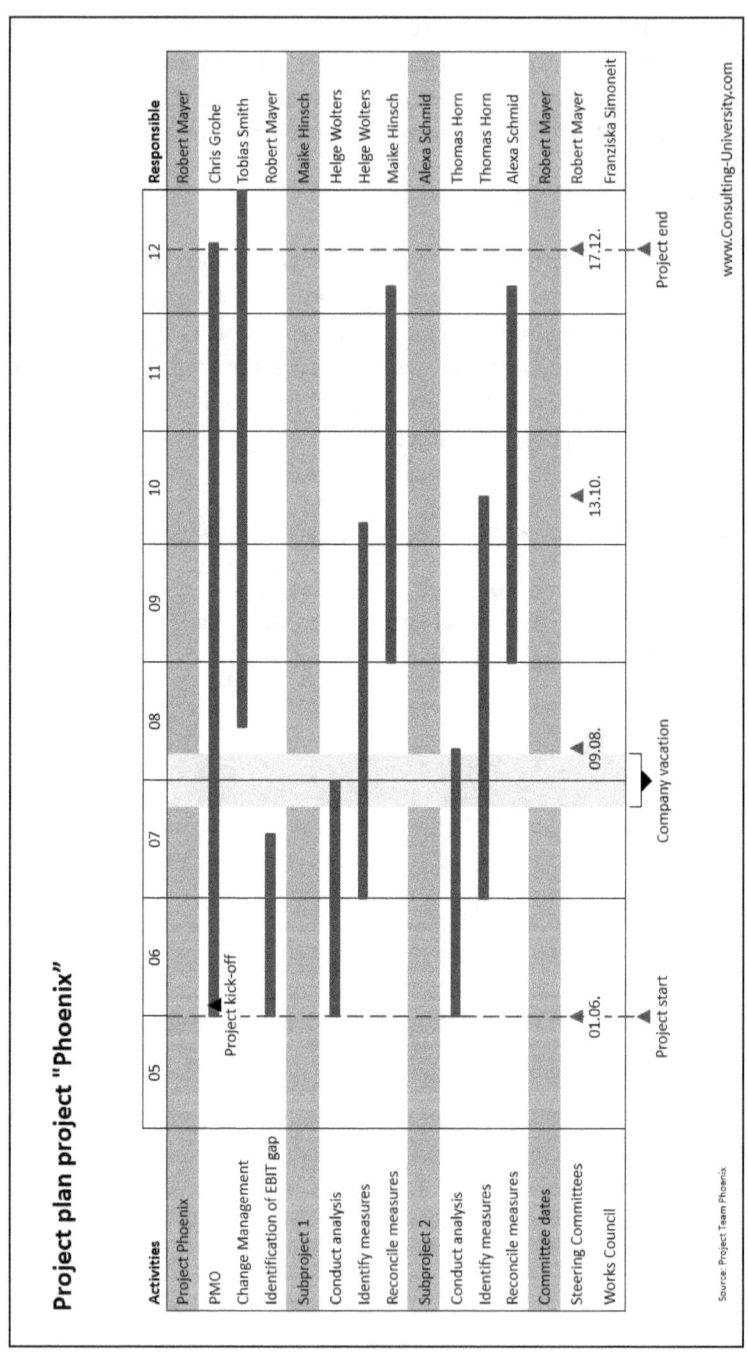

Project plan project "Phoenix"

Activities	05	06	07	08	09	10	11	12	Responsible
Project Phoenix									Robert Mayer
PMO		Project kick-off							Chris Grohe
Change Management									Tobias Smith
Identification of EBIT gap									Robert Mayer
Subproject 1									Maike Hinsch
Conduct analysis									Helge Wolters
Identify measures									Helge Wolters
Reconcile measures									Maike Hinsch
Subproject 2									Alexa Schmid
Conduct analysis									Thomas Horn
Identify measures									Thomas Horn
Reconcile measures									Alexa Schmid
Committee dates									Robert Mayer
Steering Committees		01.06.		09.08.		13.10.		17.12.	Robert Mayer
Works Council		Project start		Company vacation				Project end	Franziska Simoneit

Source: Project Team Phoenix.

www.Consulting-University.com

58

"The most important things are already included in the project plan: Who does what by when. It's good that we use think-cell[14] in the company. Project plans can be created and adapted quickly. In addition, it is still important to differentiate between responsibility for results and execution, as this can lie with different people. The subproject manager is responsible for the subproject results. However, the execution responsibility may lie with his project team member in the subproject for the measures he agrees on," Michael explained. "To show vacation times on a project plan is a technicality that things will slow down in the project at that time because many people will be on vacation," Michael added.

"Then I should be well positioned for all aspects concerning the project organization. Or are you still missing something?" Robert asked.

"You're well set up. Next, I would define the project reporting and project continuation criteria," Michael said.

"I still wanted to set up the project reporting, but why would I define project continuation criteria?" Robert asked.

Michael looked at his watch. "Oh! I'm about to have an appointment with the Strategy Head! I can explain that to you later," Michael said excitedly, grabbed his laptop, and ran to his appointment.

———

Learning Nuggets

○ Every project (or program) needs a project manager. Sounds obvious, but this is not always the case and only responsible persons for the respective sub-projects are named, but no central overall project manager.
○ The Project Management Office (PMO) should only perform PMO tasks and not contribute to the content of the project. Individual employees from the PMO will have a hard time with the content work if they control the project employees as PMO and are dependent on their cooperation for the content work.

---

[14] https://www.think-cell.com/de/ think-cell is a very good PowerPoint addon software that I can personally recommend. All major management consultancies work with think-cell in Germany and across the world.

o Efficiency in operational project work can be significantly increased using specifications and standards. Therefore, many specifications must be made to promote transparency and efficiency in the project.

o Many slides from the project organization should only be created once so that they can be used for further appointments (for example, project kick-off or first steering committee).

o With the help of defined project roles, each project member knows what is expected of them.

o The definition of the committees, including responsibilities, clarifies early in the project who is responsible for committee preparation, execution, and follow-up so that misunderstandings are avoided.

o The work mode and project rules provide standards, methods, and a framework for the project and relieve the project manager and PMO.

  o The storage location for project files (e.g., an MS SharePoint) must be defined. Depending on the version of MS SharePoint, it makes sense to define a file naming convention, so that you as the project manager know which file and which version it is.

  o An example: Date_Version_Abbreviation of the editor_Filename = "260421_01_FRK_Riskmanagement Phoenix".

o The project plan defines for everyone: "who does what by when" to avoid delays.

—

Learning nuggets for long-running projects

o Particularly in the case of long-running projects and programs, it is important to review and adjust the regular project team appointments and meetings from time to time. Meeting zombies that everyone has in their diary, but no one attends are of no help to anyone. Especially if appointments are always canceled by everyone, it is important to question the series of appointments or to act as a project manager and make the appointment a mandatory appointment (and escalate it if necessary).

o In the case of very large projects and programs, it is worthwhile to limit the number of participants and duration of the regular meetings.

- Caution: Inexperienced (sub)project managers often try to make decisions or take risks that exceed their competence, thinking that it may be interpreted as their weakness. Therefore, it must be determined early in the project who is responsible for decisions in the case of a conflict (see rules for decision-making in Chapter 7).
- Many project managers do not use the steering committee to get the needed decisions for the project or to show the possible options. Use the steering committee as a tool and steer the steering committee so that you get the decisions you need as a project manager. Do not see the steering committee only as an instrument of control and reconciliation!

———

Checklist

- Project roles and responsibilities are defined.
- Committees and responsibilities are defined.
- Appointments and meetings are defined in the project and set.
- Working mode and project rules are formulated:
    - Permissions and accesses for the project tools have been requested.
    - Appropriate tools were prepared and set up, e.g., an MS SharePoint was provided for the project and prepared by the PMO.
    - File naming and version conventions are defined.
    - Documentation standards are defined.
- Project plan (who does what by when) is written and reconciled within the project.

6. Define project reporting and project continuation criteria

When Michael came back into the office, Robert immediately asked him, "Well, did you still make it on time? The head of strategy hates nothing more than unpunctuality or not being prepared," he laughed and looked at Michael.

"All good, I just made it on time. Let's get back to your question about why you need 'project continuation criteria' in the project," Michael said and started his laptop.

Robert nodded at him, "Exactly. I've never heard of that being defined beforehand in any projects. Of course, projects were canceled here and there too, but that resulted from the current project situation," Robert explained.

"I will explain the reasons to you later and start with the project reporting because then you will see, why I like defining project continuation criteria," Michael said, showing Robert a slide on his laptop.

Project Reporting "Phoenix"
Subproject: XY

Status as of dd.mm.yyyy `Green`

Subproject status

- Results & measures taken

Current risks and countermeasures

- Risks and (possible) countermeasures

Next steps

- Next steps & measures for next reporting period

Decision applications

- Decision requests for the project manager or the steering committee

Source: Project Team Phoenix

www.Consulting-University.com

"As a project manager, why do you regularly have your subproject managers give you the status quo on their subprojects?" Michael asked.

"To identify risks early and define and take countermeasures," Robert replied.

Michael nods. "Exactly! Your goal is to identify risks for the timeline, the budget, and the quality early on so you can counteract and still get the project to the finish line," Michael said.

He continued, "One of your defined regular appointments to track this in a meaningful way is to present the weekly results. Of course, you can use a tool or software, such as Jira or Trello, based on which these aspects are discussed in the appointment. It's all just another method and especially a matter of taste," he paused for a moment and then continued:

"As a project manager, however, it is important to get a regular overview of the current status quo of the subprojects. It doesn't matter whether this is done weekly or every three to four weeks as part of sprints in an agile project methodology. Based on the status, I can see whether the project is on track or not. Many companies use percentages or Harvey Balls for this purpose. However, in my opinion, this is a complete nonsense. Every subproject manager will show progress, no matter what has happened, just to avoid being called out. In a project, a measure is either finished or it is not. This indication of "finished" or "not finished" allows you to ask further questions to the responsible person.

Therefore, it is much more important for a project manager to be able to understand in terms of content how much of the work packages have already been completed and whether the subproject still sees itself on track. Hence the indication of the project status."

"With this template, you're allowing the subproject to bring forward risks and needed decisions early on, as these are the quickest to cause delays if they're not indicated and addressed promptly," Michael explained.

"I see," Robert said and nodded. "So, you're using the reporting template to ask the subproject managers questions in the meeting to see if it deserves a green status?" Robert asked.

"Exactly. At the same time, such a report, which you should save as a PDF on the project SharePoint, serves as documentation of when risks and decision requests were made to you. This helps you as the overall project manager too, as no one can later claim, 'But I told you that and you didn't do anything!'

You always document everything. Especially if you have external service providers and consulting companies in the project, this reporting serves as a communication platform. The steering committee you can use this as documentation or as I like to say 'cover my a**' to show the steering committee the countermeasures.

As I said, it doesn't matter if this is done in MS PowerPoint like here or with a software tool. Personally, however, these points on the template are important points to me as a project manager. In addition, you can check with the 'Next steps' whether sufficient planning has been done and whether your comments have been considered by the project," Michael explained.

"Okay, I get it, but what do I need project continuation criteria for?" Robert asked.

"Okay. What do you do as a project manager when all subprojects run into a red status?" Michael asked.

"You define and implement countermeasures," Robert replied confidently.

"Okay. Another question: the project does not get out of the status 'red'. The goals are far away. As a result, the project is rescheduled and reapproved by the steering committee so that it is back to a "green" status. Within two months, it is then all "red" again compared to the updated and reapproved project plan. When is the time for you as a project manager to admit that the project has failed?" Michael asked.

Robert rolled his eyes, leaned back in his office chair, and looked at the ceiling.

"When do I admit that the project failed?" muttered Robert. "Good question, I would decide that on a project-by-project basis," Robert replied and looked at Michael again.

"Okay, that is one possibility. But why not rather define the steering committees as quality gates and define criteria for a possible project continuation as well as continuation criteria in advance? Nobody is helped if a project is continued without sense and reason. In addition, the criteria help you as a project manager in a project crisis.

In the steering committee, you can then suggest that, according to the not met project continuation criteria, now would be the time to terminate the project. The steering committee can still disagree with this, but as a project manager, you are off the hook. The steering committee can decide, what to do and if they want to escalate any measures.

Inexperienced project managers often try to somehow clarify decisions and risks that exceed their competence, thinking that it will be interpreted as a weakness. Therefore, it must be clarified early in the project who is responsible for decisions in the event of risks and conflicts and when a project is terminated. So why not instrumentalize the steering committee for this?" Michael asked.

"So, what do you think these project continuation criteria could look like on my restructuring project?" Robert asked. Michael showed him the following scribble:

Project continuation criteria are defined for each phase of the project

1st steering committee 09.08.2023

- Measures identified with the potential of at least 4% EBIT-margin of ABC Ltd.
- ...

2. steering committee 13.10.2023

- Measures identified with the potential of at least 6% EBIT-margin of ABC Ltd.
- ...

3. steering committee 17.12.23

- Measures identified with the potential of at least 6% EBIT-margin of ABC Ltd.
- ...

Premises

Measures only count from absolute volume ≥ 100 K€

Measures must be implemented by 31.06.2024

Costs for implementation of measures are to be offset against the potential[1]

1 | Excluding severance costs for personnel measures
Source: Project Team Phoenix

"If the potential is below €X million or 6% of the EBIT margin in the analysis phase, it is no longer any use talking about a restructuring project. If this happens, the project must be escalated and, if necessary, other areas that have not been part of the project scope so far must be included. Otherwise, your project will fail.

Once the measures have been designed, there should still be €X million in the potential to make the project worthwhile in terms of personnel costs. If the CFO, i.e., Dr. Haupt, disagrees, you can ask him or Ms. Simoneit how high the savings potential must be for him or her. Anything less than €1 million would be a waste of time in my opinion. In that case, Dr. Haupt would have to think about other measures, such as selling the company," Michael explained.

Robert nodded. "I hadn't thought about that at all. Especially since Dr. Haupt is part of the steering committee. He will ask Ms. Simoneit what other measures she proposes if we do not find enough."

Michael nodded.

"So, I will have the project continuation criteria approved by the first steering committee. If the steering committee does not approve these criteria, I'm still fine," Robert said.

"Yes. I know that this is a very formal act and many projects here in the company are not very formal. But once that's defined, approved, and documented, you're fine as a project manager. As a good project manager, you can always present other options for the continuation of the project. But these criteria can save a lot of time.

Either way, you're fine with the steering committee as project manager, especially since the effort is very small," Michael explained.

"What do you think would be other project continuation criteria that should be used in other projects?" Robert asked.

"If innovation projects exceed a budget in the amount of X €.

If you develop new business models in the project and the business case shows that the EBIT margin is below X% or the business case is still negative after X years.

If you are developing a new product and the development time exceeds the target value of X years.

Or as in your restructuring project, if not enough measures are identified or the EBIT margin would remain below X% despite the implemented measures," Michael explained.

"Now I've got it. And I think I'm well positioned for the first steering committee" Robert said.

"Yes, you are and now, I would prepare the entire presentation for the first steering committee and set up the rules for decision-making. Certainly, something you should reconcile with Timo. But I would prepare it. I'd be happy to scribble something for you," Michael laughed.

"Yes, with pleasure! If I have any questions, I'll get back to you!" Robert said.

Learning Nuggets

o   A decent project reporting, whether in MS PowerPoint or a software tool, gives you as a project manager the opportunity to get deep into the content of the subprojects and provide substantial comments and feedback.
o   Project continuation criteria help you as a project manager when the project becomes difficult. Pre-defined and agreed-upon project continuation criteria also protect the company's interests, as projects will only continue if the project is on track or does not become obsolete.
o   Avoid a so-called "watermelon reporting": the status "green" is displayed although the project is "red". Therefore, I am not a friend of percentages or Harvey Balls that are not clearly defined.

Checklist

o   Define project reporting and prepare it for the project with a small explanation of what you value as a project manager.

o   Define project continuation criteria and quality gates (e.g., the steering committee).

o   Have the project continuation criteria approved by the steering committee members in the first steering committee. If necessary, show why this is necessary (e.g., to avoid the project exceeding timelines or budgets).

7. Prepare and conduct the first steering committee

Michael was working on a presentation when Robert suddenly stood in front of his desk. "Do you have a few minutes to explain your scribbles on the steering committee to me?" Robert asked.

"Of course, how can I help you?" Michael asked.

"I like the ideas!" Robert replied and continued, "But I haven't used slides like this in any projects before. Can you explain them to me briefly?" He showed Michael the slide:

Rules for decision-making within the steering committee are defined and agreed upon

Composition of the steering committee

The steering committee shall be composed of four (4) people:

- The permanent, voting representatives of the management are: First Name Last Name, First Name Last Name, First Name Last Name ...
- The permanent, voting representatives of the department are: First Name Last Name, First Name Last Name ...
- Other non-voting members are: First Name Last Name, First Name Last Name ...

Criteria for the quorum of the steering committee

The steering committee can make decisions within the framework of regular meetings and, if necessary, extraordinary meetings, if all the following conditions are met:

- There are at least three (3) of the four (4) members present (or digitally connected) for regular project decisions.

Making decisions by the steering committee

- Project decisions (according to the decision-making powers of the body) are usually made by absolute majority, i.e., more than 50% of the present (or digitally connected), voting steering committee members must vote in favor of an option.
- (Optional: However, one (1) representative of the board of management must always agree).

Documentation of decisions made

- The decisions and their correctness (fulfillment of the above-mentioned criteria) are documented in the minutes of the steering committee.
- The minutes of the meeting will be sent to the members of the steering committee afterwards. If no objections are raised by the steering committee members not present at the meeting within (3) days (date of dispatch plus two days), decisions are deemed to be accepted. Otherwise, they will be resubmitted to the steering committee for decision at the following meeting.

"Sure! Before a project officially begins its operational work, i.e., before the project kick-off, I as project manager always hold a first steering committee with all members of the steering committee and especially with the project sponsor. This is the first steering committee before the project officially begins. This very formal act aids the project later, by supporting the implementation and by enforcing decisions within the organization or across organizational boundaries.

For this purpose, some project contents are defined by the steering committee members in the first steering committee:

- The rules for a quorum of the steering committee are approved,
- Project objectives, project scope, and mandating of the project or project team are approved,
- Required resources (budget and staff) are approved,
- The project organization (committees and project plan) is approved.

Especially in your restructuring project, which works across organizational and company boundaries, it is important to define and document these aspects precisely," Michael said, referring to the slide.

"During the stakeholder analysis of the committees, we already identified in advance which decisions have to be made by the steering committee during the course of the project and whether the steering committee members would be able to make these decisions.

The whole point of this is to have the right members on your project steering committee. By right members I mean, the members affected and the members, who can decide and help implement decisions. If this is not the case for one of your projects, the composition of the steering committee members must be changed. This helps you to anticipate project delays at an early stage of the project and to take them into account in the project plan. It also reduces the likelihood of canceling the project by ensuring that the steering committee can make and implement all the needed decisions.

As I said, establishing a quorum is a very formal act. Nevertheless, I can recommend it to you for projects across company borders. It helps to avoid unnecessary and time-consuming coordination during the project across company boundaries," Michael explained, tapping on the screen of the laptop.

"If the steering committee doesn't have a quorum, it inevitably leads to project delays or even project cancellation," Robert said, shaking his head.

"Exactly. And now imagine that you are running a project with external service providers, e.g., management consultants. Every internal project delay leads to budget requests from the consultants because the reasons for the delays are beyond their control. A project can very quickly suffer financial shipwreck," Michael laughed.

Robert nodded. "Do you have any other tips for the steering committee?" he asked.

"To anticipate comments within the steering committee itself, you need to send the documents to the steering committee members in advance and ask for feedback: Does anything need to be explicitly changed? Otherwise, you have the first project delay before the project has even started," Michael laughed.

Robert packed up his laptop and sat back down in his seat as Michael was saying, "And don't forget to send the minutes to everyone after the steering committee. Good documentation is important."

Learning Nuggets

o A project is only as good as the decisions that are made and implemented. To ensure this, a first steering committee must be held before the project begins, in which the rules for decision-making are defined. This is particularly important if several companies or external service providers are involved.

o In the case of very critical projects, it makes sense to meet the steering committee participants in separate interviews or meetings before the steering committee. During the interview, you can discuss and agree on critical aspects of the project. This avoids confrontational discussions in the steering committee that do not lead to the desired results. In general, it is always a good idea to meet the project sponsor and other steering committee members in advance of each steering committee and to agree on critical issues in advance.

———

Checklist

o Define rules for decision-making for the steering committee.
o Coordinate and set a date for the first steering committee including other steering committees with steering committee members and especially the project sponsor.
   o At the same time, ask for a date for the project kick-off, which the project sponsor should attend, to communicate the expectations to the project team (see Chapter 9 " Prepare, conduct, and follow up on the project kick-off ").
o Send the entire first steering committee presentation to all steering committee members in advance (at least five business days) so that there is sufficient time to receive feedback before the steering committee.
o If necessary, hold a meeting to pre-coordinate content with steering committee members.
o Document the first steering committee by sending the final steering committee presentation and minutes to all steering committee members with a request for feedback by three working days. While this has already been written into the rules of decision-making, a brief reminder with a deadline helps.

8. Additional tips before starting the project

That afternoon Robert returned to the office with his laptop and a notepad. He looked visibly relieved.

"Well, how did the first steering committee go?" Michael asked curiously.

"Really good. Dr. Haupt liked the rules for decision-making. He asked Timo to establish that as a standard for all future projects. After the steering committee, I told Timo that the idea came from you," Robert said, beaming with joy.

"Oh, very cool! Maybe then I can develop a standard slide for such meetings that we can roll out throughout the company," Michael said.

"Exactly," Robert laughed. "Do you have any last tips for me before I prepare for the project kick-off?" Robert asked.

Michael thought for a moment and then agreed. "It's always worth having a critical exchange about the project with a work colleague who questions aspects and asks the right questions. The more experience the 'project coach' has in managing projects, the better. But you're already doing that with me." Michael and Robert laughed.

"From the beginning of the project, try to develop an open, transparent project culture with a lot of personal responsibility among the project team members. This will save you a lot of work as a project manager and direct your focus to the important aspects of the project. A project lunch or a joint lunch in the canteen at the project kick-off helps to establish a corresponding project culture and to get to know the project team members better. In addition, you create a space for employees to develop, get involved, and perhaps even rediscover the fun at work that was lost in the line work," said Michael.

Robert nodded. "Yes, I've seen that in my past projects as well. The project manager is in control of the project culture, which can also tip quickly if project members are pitted against each other."

"Yes, that's why I liked being a project manager in management consulting: lots of motivated colleagues." Michael laughed. "Oh, one more thing: Before you start the project, you still have to set up risk management. I already have an idea that you can use. Even if you don't need it directly, it will help you anticipate potential risks early on and initiate countermeasures," Michael explained. "I'll send you the scribble right away.

In addition, you should already schedule a 'Lessons Learned Workshop' or a 'Debrief' at the end of the project. This offers you, as project manager, the opportunity to collect feedback and to constantly improve yourself using constructive feedback."

———

Learning Nuggets

o   A project coach can help you with critical issues and challenges during your project. It should be someone with whom you have a trusting relationship and who does not work on the project. Depending on the confidentiality level, be careful whom you choose as a project coach.
o   An appropriate project culture creates room for employees to develop. Reflect on your experience as a project member and consider what you would have wished differently or better.
o   The earlier you set up risk management, the earlier you can anticipate risks and initiate countermeasures.

———

Checklist

o   Find a project coach or mentor with whom you can confidently share ideas and risks about the project.

o   Think about what the project culture should look like in your project and live it from the beginning. Remember former project leaders with whom you enjoyed working. Remember, you don't always have to be in the spotlight as a project manager. Success is always celebrated together.

o   Set up risk management before the project begins so that you are prepared when the first risks arise.

o   Schedule a "lessons learned workshop" after project completion early in the project so you can learn and grow through constructive feedback.

9. Prepare, conduct, and follow up on the project kick-off

Michael was analyzing some competitor data on new business models when Robert came into the office. He started his laptop and grabbed a coffee. After drinking it, he looked past his monitors at Michael.

"Michael, do you have some time for me later? I need some feedback for my project kick-off presentation," Robert said.

"Well, sure. When is the project kick-off?" Michael asked.

"The project kick-off is in a week," Robert replied.

"And Dr. Haupt is participating too?" Michael asked

"Yes. The project is very important to him, and he wants to take the opportunity to explain the project goals and his expectations to all project members. I also think that's why I haven't had any cancellations from the project team for the project kick-off so far," Robert laughed.

"That's great! The project sponsor should always participate in the project kick-off. Unfortunately, this is not always the case or is difficult to implement in terms of time. I think it is very appreciative, but also important, that Dr. Haupt participates in the project kick-off during a restructuring project. I would also escalate this immediately if a project employee thinks that something else is more important than this project kick-off. Sure, private reasons can always get in the way, but this is your chance as a project manager to get everyone together on the project. Just send me your kick-off presentation and I'll give you feedback," Michael said.

***

After lunch with the entire in-house consulting team, Michael sat down at his laptop. Shortly before they left, Robert had sent him the presentation for the project kick-off. He looked through the presentation, added his feedback including further slide ideas, and then sent it back to Robert, who was promptly back at Michael's desk.

Michael looked at Robert, "Well, I guess you have some questions concerning my feedback?"

Robert nodded. "Yes, in my opinion, you made the project kick-off too operational. After all, Dr. Haupt is involved as the project sponsor and CFO, so I wanted to reach his level," Robert replied.

"I understand that. That's why I would split the appointment according to the agenda into two parts," Michael said, pointing to the agenda.

Agenda

TOP	Content	Presenter
1	**Goals and project scope of Project Phoenix**	**Dr. Haupt**
2	Project organization Phoenix	Mr. Mayer
3	Roles, work mode and project rules	Mr. Mayer
4	Project plan and next steps	Mr. Mayer

"The project kick-off is your chance as a project manager to transparently present all operational aspects of the project, define standards and answer the questions of the project members. This appointment must be kept very operational so that templates and software tools are presented and explained, even if the project sponsor is present.

After all, it is enough for Dr. Haupt to be present as the project sponsor for the first part of the agenda, to communicate his goals and expectations, and to present the relevance of the project to all participants. You can tell him, that he can happily stay for the rest of the kick-off, but this will be very operational topics for the project team.

The aim of the project kick-off is, that all project members can start straight away with the project after the kick-off. This means that every project member knows what is expected of him and how he must work," Michael explained.

"That's a good idea. I'll give him the option if he's present for the whole appointment. But his presence is only relevant for the first section," Robert said.

"Exactly. Believe me, as a CFO, he's happy if he doesn't have to be present for the whole two hours. You can bring that up with his secretary when you make the appointment, or you can take him aside just before the appointment and discuss it with him. You can tell him, that the kick-off will get very operational after his part and that his presence is good for the project, but not necessary. Now he has two easy options and knows that his valuable time will not be wasted," Michael explained to Robert, who nodded in response.

"Michael, you added a slide for the status reporting too. Can you tell me a few words about it?" Robert said, pointing to the slide.

The overall project can only have the status of the subprojects

Project status definitions

There are deviations in terms of time, budget, and results. Countermeasures were unsuccessful. There is a need for action in the project.

There are deviations in terms of time, budget, and results. Countermeasures to achieve the goals and milestones have been or will be taken.

There are no deviations from the plan in terms of time, budget, and results. All goals and milestones will be achieved according to plan.

Michael laughed: "This is one of my favorite slides at the beginning of every project. As a project manager, I like to show and explain it during the kick-off. All the subproject managers need to know when they need to set the status for their subproject to 'yellow' or 'red.'

In addition, it has to be clear to all project members, that the status of the project cannot exceed the status of a subproject."

"So, if a subproject has a yellow status, then the entire project has a yellow status?" asked Robert.

"Exactly. And if a sub-project is 'red', then the entire project is 'red'. Logically, the entire project can't deliver on time, quality, and cost if a subproject cannot ensure that.

Sure, some people will want to argue with me now, but that's how I see it.

Of course, the subproject managers usually don't like this definition. For example, if the steering committee asks why the project has the overall status 'yellow' and you as the project manager refer to a subproject, then this is not beneficial for the subproject manager.

At the same time, it increases his responsibility as a subproject manager, which he needs to be aware of. If he doesn't deliver as a subproject manager, the whole project can be delayed in terms of cost, time, and quality," Michael said.

"Therefore, the decision and escalation sequence in the project should be clear to everyone. Certainly, this is clear to any experienced project member. Yet I would always show these slides in the kick-off. It avoids unnecessary questions within the project and clarifies your standards for the project from the beginning," Michael continued, pointing to a slide in the backup:

Decision and escalation process for the Phoenix project

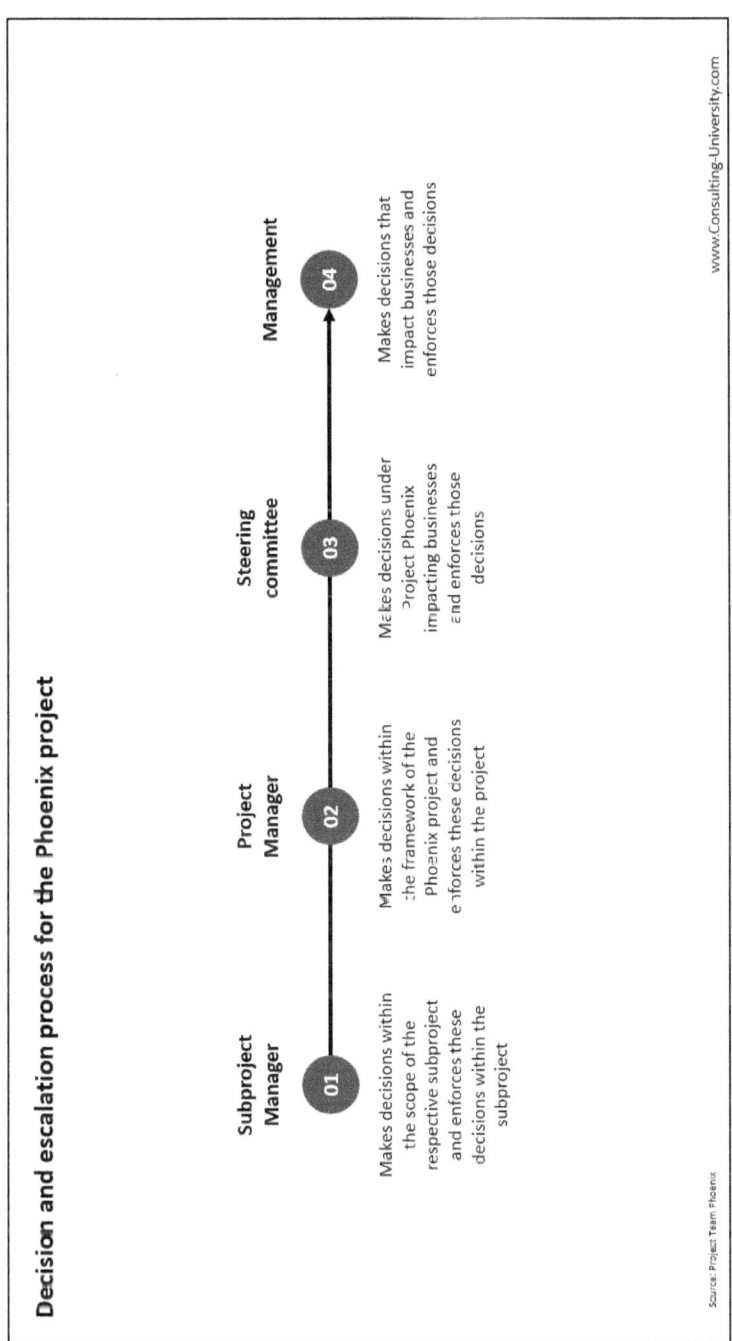

Subproject Manager

01

Makes decisions within the scope of the respective subproject and enforces these decisions within the subproject

Project Manager

02

Makes decisions within the framework of the Phoenix project and enforces these decisions within the project

Steering committee

03

Makes decisions under Project Phoenix impacting businesses and enforces those decisions

Management

04

Makes decisions that impact businesses and enforces those decisions

"You're right, I'll show them at the project kick-off and explain them briefly," Robert said. "Apart from that, I do not have any further questions about your feedback. Thanks!" Robert picked up his laptop and sat back down at his desk.

"Don't forget to send the presentation to all project members after the kick-off. In addition, I always recommend taking minutes, if anything changes. This will act as the official 'GO' to the project as well", Michael added as Robert plugged in his laptop.

Robert nodded and began working on the kick-off slides to send them to all project members in advance.

——

Learning Nuggets

o The project sponsor should try and attend the project kick-off to highlight the relevance of the project.
o Apart from that, the project kick-off must be kept very operational, so that the project members can start with the project straight away.
o The more standards you define in advance, the faster the project can start and the less likely you will face any time-consuming questions during the project.

——

Checklist

o The project sponsor is invited to the project kick-off.
  o Depending on the company size and the level of the project sponsor, coordinate the meeting with his or her assistant or directly with him or her.
  o Make sure the project sponsor is clear on that to communicate. Focus on the project goals and expectations.
o The project kick-off presentation should be sent to all project team members at least 48 hours before the meeting so that they can review the slides in advance and provide constructive feedback at the meeting or ask questions.

- The presentation contains all standards of the project organization as well as other relevant slides so that the project team can start straight away with the project work directly afterward.
- After the project kick-off, the updated presentation with the minutes is sent to all project members and stored centrally for everyone on the project SharePoint (or equivalent).

Starting the project

After the project kick-off, Robert came back to the office beaming with joy. "Michael, it went great. Thanks for your feedback and all the support! Dr. Haupt was very pleased with the preparation and even mentioned this to Timo on his way out," Robert said and put everything down on his desk.

"Next, I will send the final presentation with the last comments from the meeting and the minutes to all participants. This marks the start of my first project as a project manager!" Robert laughed. You could see that he was very pleased with all the positive feedback.

"Oh, and Timo knows you're my project coach for the project, by the way," Robert laughed. "I have spoken with him and will use these slides as a template for further projects," Robert said.

"Very good," Michael said and smiled back at Robert.

***

All provided slides are an example and need to be adapted to your company and your project specifics. However, they give you a good and comprehensive insight into how to prepare and start your projects.

I hope that my book was able to help you. You can find all slides as a download on my website www.Consulting-Universtiy.com

Of course, the start of the project is not the end of the story and now the operational project work begins. Look at the book series "Consulting-University.com" on Amazon. New books will come out until the end of this and next year.

Add-on: Unlocking the potential of ChatGPT

If you are starting to work in project management or if you are an experienced project manager, ChatGPT and other AI tools can help you with certain use cases and save time. I wrote an article, named "Unlocking the Potential of ChatGPT in Project Management: 8 easy use-cases", about this on Medium.com and my blog. On Medium.com my article got over 1.200 Views after publishing it (https://medium.com/p/c3fd7cff8466). To help you get started with ChatGPT in project management, I would like to introduce the following prompts. I used these prompts on ChatGPT https://chat.openai.com/

1. Brainstorm ideas for workshops and meetings

"Give me 10 creative ideas to start a workshop."

"Give me 10 creative ideas to start a project kick-off "

If you are trying to impress your clients or colleagues at a meeting, why not ask ChatGPT to brainstorm some innovative ideas to start a workshop or a project kick-off?

2. Create market reports

"Please act as a business consultant and generate a report on the current state of the e-commerce market for bicycles and provide insights on potential growth opportunities for our business. Structure these findings in 5 PowerPoint charts including action titles and three bullets per slide."

Do you want to convince your boss of a new business opportunity, or a strategic move or you are looking for an opener for your project? Why not create a short market report? I highly recommend checking any numbers, so you can name a reliable data source. Btw. you can make the tool act as somebody, e.g., a business consultant, and get corresponding answers.

3. Identify basics for a new project

"What are the 10 major KPIs for the automotive industry?"

"Write a list of the top 10 automotive brands according to how many cars they have sold and revenue. Please put it into a table."

"Write a list of the top 10 Chinese automotive brands."

If you are entering a new industry or a new department, it is always good to know, what is important for them and talk in their language. Besides getting a market report, you can ask for specific industry knowledge, like common KPIs or competitor lists. In addition, this knowledge can save you from asking stupid questions in a meeting, revealing you as a newbie.

4. Brainstorm actual project tasks

"Brainstorm 10 innovative and creative ideas to cut logistic costs at a retail company."

"What measures have retail companies undertaken in the last 5 years, to cut costs?"

„Name 10 Project management tools, which have good ratings and customer feedback. Add their homepage and put it into a table."

If you got a task from your boss and do not know, where to start, why not ask ChatGPT (or google it)? Even if 9 out of 10 ideas are not suitable for your company, there will still be this one idea, which only took you a minute to research. In addition, you can always ask the AI tool to come up with further ideas and use them as a starting point for your further research on specific topics.

5. Manage project risks

"Please answer as a business consultant: In my projects steering committee, the stakeholders never make any decisions. Do you have any solutions?"

Imagine you are a project manager and have a project risk, you do not know how to handle. Why not get some solutions from an AI tool? As the project manager, you will still have to analyze the problem and identify a suitable solution. But the tool can help you in case you get stuck with project management issues and project risks!

6. Create an agenda for a Steering committee and other meetings

"How does the agenda for a project steering committee look like?"

As this might be basic project management skills for some people, this can be gold for a junior consultant, a junior project manager, or somebody new to the world of project management. This prompt can give you a general idea of an agenda to many meetings, you may have never participated in.

7. Translate text into another language

"Translate the article into German."

ChatGPT can translate your documents and text. This will save you time if you are communicating with stakeholders in different languages. Although ChatGPT can translate, I prefer Deepl.com as it can translate whole MS PowerPoint presentations into different languages. This makes it even easier and saves even more time.

8. Generate pre-written E-mails

"Can you please write a friendly but formal E-mail to my co-workers, inviting them to our project kick-off? Date: 13th of March 2023. Time: 2–4 pm. Location: Great Hall."

While you might prefer to write these by yourself, it is a pain for many. ChatGPT can be used to generate personalized email templates. This can save you time and improve your communication skills with clients and stakeholders.

About me, Frederick King

I want to take a moment to share a glimpse into my journey as a project manager and author. Throughout my professional career, I have been fortunate to gather a lot of experience and insights, which have shaped my perspective on project management and consulting within corporate environments:

- Over a decade of experience in consulting with over 25 conducted projects,
- Project Manager at Porsche Consulting,
- Senior Consultant at PwC (PricewaterhouseCoopers),
- Experience on international projects in England, Italy, Germany, and Saudi Arabia,
- Freelance project manager since 2020.

But it wasn't all smooth sailing. Like any project manager, I encountered hurdles and setbacks along the way. It was during the project implementation phase that I experienced firsthand the consequences of insufficient project planning and project preparation. Lessons learned from these experiences became a catalyst for my determination to help you avoid similar pitfalls.

Writing became a natural outlet for sharing my knowledge and experiences. In addition to this book, I have authored a total of four books on project management and innovation management, each one born out of a desire to contribute to the professional growth of project managers and consultants. I am also proud to have established www.consulting-university.com, where I take deep dives into topics of consulting, innovation management, and project management, providing a platform for continuous learning and exchange of ideas.

As a freelance project manager, I have had the privilege of working with major clients who understand the significance of a well-structured project setup. They often engage my services to ensure strong project planning, effective project preparation, and seamless project kick-offs. It brings me immense satisfaction to witness the positive impact that these steps have on the trajectory of their projects and programs.

In my practice as a project manager, I adhere to a guiding principle that has served me well throughout my career: taking personal responsibility. When mistakes or risks arise, I always look inward first, examining my work and actions. As the project manager, I believe it is crucial to recognize that the project is ultimately my responsibility, regardless of the client or the organization for which I am working.

I would like to leave you with a quote that encapsulates a principle close to my heart: "Don't let the fun in the project be overshadowed". Cherish the human aspect of your projects, for a shared cup of coffee or a team dinner, can work wonders in fostering friendship and healing any project-related tensions.

I wish you all the best in your future endeavors as project managers and consultants. Feel free to connect with me on LinkedIn

https://www.linkedin.com/in/freddi-king/

or have a look at my website, where you will find my blog, and all provided templates to download:

www.Consulting-University.com

Kind regards,

Frederick

PS If you liked this book, feel free to recommend it to your friends, colleagues and please do write a review on Amazon. I'm particularly interested in which chapters or aspects helped you most. This gives me a good indication of what I need to focus on in the future to support you.

Appendix

I. List of abbreviations

€	Euro (currency)
C&C	Change & Communication
CFO	Chief Financial Officer
EBIT	Earnings before interest and taxes
e.g.	Example given
FTE	Full-time equivalent (FTE)
K€	Thousand euros
i.e.	in the example
INC	Inhouse Consulting
Ltd.	Limited liability company (legal form)
MS	Microsoft
PMO	Project Management Office
OU	Organizational unit or department/company
SMART	specific, measurable, attractive, realistic, scheduled.
dd.mm.yyyy	Date format: Day. Month. Year.

II. Statements and References

II.I Problem, objective, solutions, and measures

To explain it, I'll use an easy example:

Problem definition: What is the problem?

- My wife is mad at me because I forgot our wedding anniversary.

Objective: What do you want to achieve?

- I want a happy wife.

Solutions: What solutions do I need to achieve the objective, a happy wife?

1   Home-cooked food
2.   Flowers

Measures: What do I need to do to achieve the solutions? (Step-by-step guide):

1.1 Shop groceries.
1.2 Cook food.
1.3 Serve food.
2.1 Buy flowers.

In the context of project work, solutions can also be a concept, an innovative business model, a process, or new software. More important than the exact definition is therefore to define what has to be implemented at the end of the project and what must be done to achieve it. Therefore, do not focus on a perfectly formulated goal in the first draft, as this can change throughout project preparation.

II.II Definition of the steering committee as a project committee

The steering committee is a decision-making and escalation committee that is superordinate to the project. It is made up of high-ranking representatives of the affected departments, the client, and, if necessary, external service providers. The steering committee makes decisions whenever a decision exceeds the competencies of the project manager, or a decision requires consensus among all participants.

If the necessary decision or escalation also exceeds the competence of the steering committee, the decision must be made within the framework of a higher committee or by the management/board meeting.

Escalation in this sense means the structured forwarding of an issue to the next higher hierarchical level if a challenge or risk cannot be resolved at the current hierarchical level.

III. Consolidated checklist for project preparation

1. Define the project objectives and scope

o   Project objectives and scope (deliverables and measures) are defined.
o   It is defined as what is not included in the project scope.
o   If needed: Interviews were conducted with all steering committee participants and relevant stakeholders regarding project goals and scope.
o   Project goals and scope are agreed upon with steering committee participants before the first steering committee.

2. Determine the project sponsor

o   The project sponsor has been named and has agreed to be the project sponsor.
o   Actual organizational charts of participating departments and companies can help you if you do not know, who will be participating in the project.

3. Identify and analyze the relevant stakeholders

o   Stakeholder analysis is conducted within the project team before the start of the project.
o   Stakeholder analysis is discussed with trustful colleagues, who can assess if there are any more stakeholders or consequences for the project.
o   Consequences and implications from the stakeholder analysis are applied and considered in further project preparation and work.

4. Define and coordinate the project resources

o   All project members have been appointed and informed accordingly about the project and their tasks.
o   Written assurance (for example, via e-mail) was obtained from the managers and supervisors for the project staff (project, name of employee, capacity, duration).
o   Budgets were requested and released as needed from the required departments.

- o If needed, a project room and additional meeting rooms were reserved for the duration of the project.
- o If necessary, the project was approved by the relevant departments (if necessary, this also happens only in the steering committee kick-off (see Chapter 7)).

5. Determine the project organization

- o Project roles and responsibilities are defined.
- o Committees and responsibilities are defined.
- o Appointments and meetings are defined in the project and set.
- o Working mode and project rules are formulated:
  - o Permissions and accesses for the project tools have been requested.
  - o Appropriate tools were prepared and set up, e.g., an MS SharePoint was provided for the project and prepared by the PMO.
  - o File naming and version conventions are defined.
  - o Documentation standards are defined.

Project plan (who does what by when) is written and reconciled within the project.

6. Define the project reporting and the project continuation criteria

- o Define project reporting and prepare it for the project with a small explanation of what you value as a project manager.
- o Define project continuation criteria and quality gates (e.g., the steering committee).
- o Have the project continuation criteria approved by the steering committee members in the first steering committee. If necessary, show why this is necessary (e.g., to avoid the project exceeding timelines or budgets).

7. Prepare and conduct the first steering committee

- o Define rules for decision-making for the steering committee.
- o Coordinate and set a date for the first steering committee including other steering committees with steering committee members and especially the project sponsor.

- At the same time, ask for a date for the project kick-off, which the project sponsor should attend, to communicate the expectations to the project team (see Chapter 9 " Prepare, conduct, and follow up on the project kick-off ").
- Send the entire first steering committee presentation to all steering committee members in advance (at least five business days) so that there is sufficient time to receive feedback before the steering committee.
- If necessary, hold a meeting to pre-coordinate content with steering committee members.
- Document the first steering committee by sending the final steering committee presentation and minutes to all steering committee members with a request for feedback by three working days. While this has already been written into the rules of decision-making, a brief reminder with a deadline helps.

8. Additional tips before starting the project

- Find a project coach or mentor with whom you can confidently share ideas and risks about the project.
- Think about what the project culture should look like in your project and live it from the beginning. Remember former project leaders with whom you enjoyed working. Remember, you don't always have to be in the spotlight as a project manager. Success is always celebrated together.
- Set up risk management before the project begins so that you are prepared when the first risks arise.
- Schedule a "lessons learned workshop" after project completion early in the project so you can learn and grow through constructive feedback.

9. Prepare, conduct, and follow up on the project kick-off

- The project sponsor is invited to the project kick-off.
  - Depending on the company size and the level of the project sponsor, coordinate the meeting with his or her assistant or directly with him or her.

- o Make sure the project sponsor is clear on that to communicate. Focus on the project goals and expectations.
- o The project kick-off presentation should be sent to all project team members at least 48 hours before the meeting so that they can review the slides in advance and provide constructive feedback at the meeting or ask questions.
- o The presentation contains all standards of the project organization as well as other relevant slides so that the project team can start straight away with the project work directly afterward.
- o After the project kick-off, the updated presentation with the minutes is sent to all project members and stored centrally for everyone on the project SharePoint (or equivalent).